Chasing the American Dyke Dream

homestretch

Chasing the American Dyke Dream

homestretch

Edited by
Susan Fox Rogers

CLEIS
PRESS

Published in the United States by Cleis Press Inc., P.O. Box 14684, San Francisco, California 94114.

Printed in the United States.
Cover design: Scott Idleman/Blink
Text design: Karen Huff
Logo art: Juana Alicia

First Edition.
10 9 8 7 6 5 4 3 2 1

Library of Congress Cataloging-in-Publication Data

Chasing the American dyke dream: homestretch / edited by Susan Fox Rogers. — 1st ed.
    p.   cm.
  ISBN 1-57344-036-1 (trade pbk. : alk. paper)
  1. Lesbians. 2. Lesbians' writings. I. Rogers, Susan Fox.
HQ75.5.A49   1998
305.48 ' 9664 — dc21   98-14274
                      CIP

Valerie Miner, "Holding on to the Day," first appeared in *The American Voice,* Volume 38, summer 1995.

"For the Straight Folks Who Don't Mind Gays but Wish They Weren't So BLATANT" by Pat Parker from *Movement in Black,* Firebrand Books, Ithaca, NY. Copyright © 1978 by Pat Parker. Permission granted by Firebrand Books.

"Quaker Meeting, the Sixties," and "A History of Sexual Preference" appear in *All-American Girl* by Robin Becker, University of Pittsburgh Press, 1996.

For my cousin, Elizabeth Fox Krohn,
who is family, and "home"

Acknowledgments

There are many people to thank when an anthology is created. First, my thanks to Frederique Delacoste at Cleis for her enthusiasm for the project and to Felice Newman and the whole Cleis team for making this into a book. There were many friends; those from the "home" that I left on the East Coast, especially Teri Condon, Alfie Guy, and the women at yoga who helped by talking and stretching with me. And now, in my new home in Tucson, there are friends who already feel like family: Deborah Jane Addis, Nancy Bissell, Boyer Rickel, Gary Kautto, and Randy Spalding. Through it all, there has been my sister Becky; the baby lions, Max P. Bear and Smudge; the moodiest dog, Babka; and Sam, who *is* home. But thanks must go mainly to the writers who worked with me over many months, sharing their stories of home. Special thanks to those nine (out of twenty-two) who did not move from one home to another during the production of this book.

"If 'home' can be anywhere, how is one to look for it, where is one to find it?"

—MAY SARTON

Contents

❧

Introduction

It's Tuesday morning, so it must be yoga day. I wake happy knowing that for an hour and a half I will journey into my body, leave manuscripts and my desk behind, maybe turn off my mind and just breath.

I roll over, kiss you, get up and make coffee while you take the dog out, the cats following you down the dirt road. I hear you yell at the dog as she chases the kittens, even though they love being chased. The four of you come back into the house in a burst of energy and even though you only have fifteen minutes to shower, get dressed, and leave for work, you head for your computer and log on, read a few messages, *The New York Times*, whatever interests you. All I know is that the internet is more important than coffee, which I deliver to you as you stare at the enormous screen, more important than the bowl of oatmeal I place to your side knowing that you'll eat only a bite or two before giving it to the dog.

Already late, you skid out the door of this house that you bought as we were meeting and falling in love. I wanted to say: don't buy that house five miles back on a dirt road with its three garages and sloping green yard. But we'd only kissed once or twice when you closed and who was I to tell you what to buy? I moved in four months after you did, and it's the first time I've felt that I've created a home with a lover.

And yet neither of us considers this house home. Your heart is back on East Hill Road, with the huge windows and landscape views, and the small studio that you built yourself to write in. My heart is back on Clove Road where overflow water ran from the pipe, and the cliffs and trails I have loved for over twenty years rise just across the road and over the valley. But here we are with pots and pans, animals, a garden that surprises us with its colors and abundance, and stability. How is it that I feel so at home in a place that isn't home?

∿

All of my thoughts on home began in my own search, which was deeply rooted in place. I spent hours revisiting the many structures of my childhood and the houses I have inhabited as an adult. That idea of home being located in a house is echoed throughout this collection. In Linda Smukler's "Colors of Home," which defies the traditional essay form with its prose poem structure, she gives a vivid portrait of several different homes she has created. These are rooted in the colors, smells, and tastes of love that reside there. Valerie Miner literally builds her house, and the work itself helps to create *home*.

Often the homes detailed in this collection are not ones we have created, but are rather those of origin: the family home. Tzivia Gover's "These Walls" describes the house that her lover is building, but sweat alone is not enough, and her thoughts keep traveling back to her childhood on Long Island. For Gover, as for many in this collection, to get at home in the present, they have had to revisit their younger selves. Some of these stories are filled with nostalgia for a place that no longer exists. When tatiana de la tierra returns to her birthplace in Colombia, the town is remarkably the same, but with the death of her aunt, that connection to the past is gone.

For many others though, the family home is what we have fled—because of violence, or from a need to come out. These homes of our families have deep closets and are not centers but places to move away from, to be avoided. Elaine Beale flees the pain of her home in Yorkshire to go to London, and then on to San Francisco. When she returns to Yorkshire much later, she realizes this is not where she belongs. Rachel Weaver describes the push and pull of home, the nostalgia and fear, the love and hate. Knowing all of this, she spends one last summer in Ohio, and her time there is juxtaposed with the rather absurd hunger strike of a local politician, Billy Inmon.

Margaret Vandenburg, in a psycho-literary search, humorously and incitefully concludes that we are "phobic" about our family homes, and that phobia can dictate—even ruin—our lives and relationships. So traditional notions of a picket fence and two-car garage are not always a part of the lesbian fantasy, and many are working hard to create their own definitions of home. That is one thing that all of these stories share: an active search. Reading the many ways that we have found or created this renewed my faith in lesbian inventiveness, creativity, and originality.

What I found fascinating was the number of manuscripts I received that explored the heartland of this country. Katia Hope Noyes travels from San Francisco—*the* lesbian homeland—to Minnesota, in search of something that seems to be deeply rooted there in the cornfields. As Elizabeth Howell notes, being geographically centered helps—to feel "centered," to write. Howell, who spent years searching for home only to return to where she started from, is deeply connected to the land of Missouri. But that territory isn't always so safe: she writes of being afraid living as a lesbian in conservative, rural country. Mary Hussmann writes of her ambivalence toward Iowa. Often she wants to just leave the house she has bought and created with family in mind. In her dreams she will buy an Airstream and head for the promise of space in Alaska.

Who among us hasn't just wanted to up and go? Live our lives on the road, never really settling down?

~~

I leave the house at eight-fifteen after letting the dog out to pee, making sure the cat food is put away so the dog won't eat it. It's these little details that drive me nuts, but they're part of what makes a home. It's like knowing which floorboards squeak, and how to get a stuck window open.

I drive to Great Barrington, just across the border in Massachusetts. There is talk in the empty, wooden-floored room, everyone catching up on the week. We don't know each other well, but the routine makes us familiar, and I care if Gabriella's son is well, if Alice's ex-husband has returned.

~~

Family: that's what makes a home. A dog, a cat, the kids. Merril Mushroom's portrait of her southern home is a place where her children think they are rich. As she repeats this refrain, we get a complex portrait of a family that loves and struggles together. For Judith Nichols, holding a home together as a lesbian mom with two kids is a juggling act made harder without a lover there to help feed and play with them, and to fix the kitchen sink. Monalesia Earle describes the emotional complexity of her mother as home, and Louise Rafkin wonders what she will call home when her mother passes away.

~e~

I hand my yoga teacher, Amy, a copy of one of my anthologies, hot off the press. I want her to know what it is I do all of the other days and hours I am not here, working toward something (toward what, I'm not entirely sure). She takes off her glasses, places the book two inches from her eyes and squints. She's nearly blind and never reads unless she has to. For some reason this is something that I love about her, that writing and reading are not a part of her life. I wonder what it would be like if I spent a day not reading manuscripts, the newspaper, letters; and not writing, in my journal, stories, email messages. What would it be like if I spent a lifetime empty of printed words? It's in words that I have always found my center, I realize now, my home. It's books, boxes filled with my journals, not clothes or old furniture that I have moved carefully, faithfully from one house to the next.

~e~

Home in words is perhaps what connects all of these pieces, but both Terry Wolverton and Robin Becker explicitly acknowledge their centers there. Wolverton's community is one of like-minded gay and lesbian artists that she has helped create in Los Angeles. It is ideas, words that bind them, and as they move from their run-down meeting space to a shiny new structure, she wonders what words will fill that new space. Poet Robin Becker travels to "Beloved Places," in the West where she can be creative, leaving home as the place where she works to make a living.

～

Amy is sitting beside me, her small body cradling mine, helping my arm to loop around the back of my body, connecting one hand with another, pushing this stretch that moves my back into new places. Her pull is definite but firm, her skin smooth and clean against my sweaty body. I smell something sweet, her deodorant or shampoo, and that makes me breathe more deeply, taking the air down deep into my lungs the way I'm supposed to. My head is turned away from her and I know that if I spun my head my lips would collide with hers and probably I would kiss her.

She releases my body and moves away. I feel my body slip back into a less stretched position and regret I wasn't able to hold it longer, feeling that stretch through my back, my arms, my hips.

The smell of food cooking rises from below and someone comments about it, and we all laugh. Suddenly we're all hungry, as we move into our next position. I begin to think about sitting in the coffee shop downtown where I will read manuscripts that have arrived for this collection, drink dark coffee, and eat a muffin too. Home is always with me, never far from my thoughts, and the manuscripts that

I carry with me wherever I go are a reminder of this. I'm not reading these manuscripts because I have to—I want to read them: they are helping me in my search, giving my ideas new dimensions. That's why I wanted to edit this collection: to explore with others, in the community of lesbian writers.

~

Some, like me, actively embark on a physical search for home. The crescendo of this search is offered in D. Killian's "This is America," as she takes a train across the United States as a homecoming gesture after many years of living abroad. What she is greeted by is America—horrifying in many ways.

It's the richness of home that fascinates me, how it's not easy, not simple. Liz Galst, in dating a goy and wrestling with family, comes to see home in her Jewishness, and the culture, language, and faith that comes with that. Lauren Crux is at home in water and so it is important that her lover—who is afraid of water—learn to swim. She needs to know that her lover will not drown in her home. L.K. Barnett and her lover find home in shared food from their pasts. And M. Paz Galupo finds home when her tongue rests in her lover's mouth.

Home is what makes us centered, happy, sexy, and alive. It also makes us cringe, run away. The home movies of our minds are offered, in all their complexity, in Vickie Reitenauer's sharp images.

~~~

"Breath," Amy says, bringing some focus back to the room, to the energy that has been building here with each breath.

"When I finally mastered this position I felt something in my lower back," she says. She's rubbing her lower back, standing tall. "I can't describe it, but it was like coming home."

I start to smile.

"Do you feel it?" Amy asks, catching my smile.

"Hardly," I say. But I want to feel this, and for the moment I am delighting in this idea of home resting in the base of my spine, in my body. I imagine stretching toward this home as have the writers in this collection. I am delighted by the flexibility of ideas and the grace of writing gathered here. I feel the stretch in this collection, a reach toward all that is inventive, new, wonderfully lesbian in perspective. And I know we're all in the homestretch, moving toward some place we can call home.

MARY HUSSMANN

~

Horizon

It's August, and I've been heading west on Interstate 80, eyeing all the motor homes, imagining how I might go north to Canada, then west to the Alcan Highway, up through the Yukon to Alaska, picking up work and living out of a cozy silver Airstream. I can see myself in Whitehorse, working behind a smoke-darkened bar, pouring shots of Yukon Jack for the shy-hearted men and brassy women. But just when I'm in the midst of figuring out how I'd swing the deal to get that little Airstream, my mind steers itself right back to Iowa. To my debts and my job and the house in Iowa City that I bought a few years ago with a down payment from my mother's estate. To the front steps that need fixing. To the broken window in the garage. With a groan I shift the yoke of responsibility and home ownership back onto my shoulders, tear my eyes from the trailers and campers, and stare down the highway ahead. It doesn't seem fair, I think, all this worry and my house isn't even half as nice as the houses of my childhood: three of them, all within blocks of each other.

I suppose each represented a step up, reflecting the growth of my father's dental practice. The first house I recall was a modest white Colonial, and my only memory is of the gaudy wallpaper with huge colored flowers: classic fifties decor. Then came the '60s and we moved into the house next door, a Tudor-esque affair with dark wood around the top and stucco around the lower level. It was bigger, and had a book-lined music room where I half-heartedly practiced on my mother's Chickering upright. Already chafing under gender roles, I hated the yellow roses on the wallpaper in my bedroom, coveting instead my brothers' wallpaper, with its scenes of rocket ships and moon craters and planets. But my favorite room was the huge kitchen, with its red linoleum floor and knotty pine walls. Though I was scolded if caught, I couldn't stop myself from poking at the gnarled knots until they fell backwards, into the dark space between the paneling and studs.

Humming along the interstate in my Jeep, my dream car, I remember that when I was twelve we moved into my mother's dream house, a sprawling Cape Cod I too would come to cherish, complete with weathered cedar shakes, twenty windows on the first floor, and a cypress roof. Old Dr. Magee, who delivered my father, built the house, and it was already forty-five years old when we moved in. When the Magees sold us the house and moved to a retirement home they left us all the books in the library. Many of them had their or their twin daughters' names pasted to bookplates inside the front covers. It bothered me as a child to read those books. I felt as if I were invading their privacy, peeking into their history. The dining room doorway had tiny notches ticking higher and higher, testifying to the Magee girls' growth. Then the notches stopped, not too much higher than where I came on the door frame. I liked to imagine the twins pounding up the basement steps, as I did after the light was turned out, afraid of the darkness hurrying behind me, or I imagined them sitting together in the bathtub, counting the little octagonal tiles in the bathroom floor.

But gradually, imperceptibly, that house became witness and repository for our family's history, just as it had for the Magees. My parents added their books to the library shelves, and my brothers' growth was documented in pencil lines on the kitchen doorway. New nicks and gouges and chipped paint appeared carrying our memories of accidents or antics. I started to mark the house as mine in bolder, more obvious ways. I took a can of spray paint from my father's workbench and wrote MARY and KOOL KAT on the basement walls, carved peace symbols and my initials into the basement stairs with my woodburning set.

For a child, home is a paradox: a place of safety and a place of enclosure. The nest I could flutter back to when hurt or lonely, yet also the place I knew deep down I'd have to leave when I grew up. With this in mind, I can only guess at my motives for taking my BB gun one Sunday afternoon when I was twelve and carefully, methodically, shooting out every single paned window in the garage when my parents were away. Was it, in some screwy Freudian way, a gesture of killing the house in order to break free, to get away? A precursor to my midlife urges to roam? All I remember was that it was utterly thrilling, the sound of all that shattering glass, the power I discovered in breaking things.

Six years ago, long after my father had died and after my youngest brother had moved out, my mother sold our house and bought another smaller one just a block down the street. Driving to Waterloo for Christmas or for a visit, I'd pull up in front of 228, our old house, and realize with a start that it wasn't ours anymore. Though I knew my mother had no use for such a large house, it seemed that the new owners were interlopers, and I was resentful. Perhaps I was resentful of her as well. "How could she?" my brother asked, "It's our *house.*" I knew what he meant; it felt as if she had sold our childhood, our history. The new owners had torn down the white picket fence I'd been forced to paint summer after summer. They weren't trimming the bushes and the shutters needed painting.

It seemed that through their neglect they were marking the house, just as I had years before, to rid it of the Magees.

My mother lived in her new home barely a year before she died, and since the house itself held no memories for us, we sold it, after dividing and disposing of her personal belongings. With the small sum of money I got after the estate was settled, I put a down payment on the house I had rented for two years with my girlfriend, Myra. Since Myra was a grad student, the issue of whether we'd buy the house together was a moot point. She couldn't afford to and I was secretly relieved. I've always been skittish about buying things beyond toothpaste or groceries with a lover. Even at thirty-six I didn't think I was ready to make the kind of commitment buying a house would imply and in retrospect it's a good thing we didn't buy it together since we later decided we were better friends than lovers. Nor was I really sure I was ready to be a homeowner, but none of my younger brothers were married at the time, and all of them rented apartments in their respective cities. As the oldest, and the only female, I think I felt some previously undiscovered need, or more likely, an obligation, to take charge as the family matriarch, and to provide a literal home base, as my mother had for the years since our father died.

For several years I held Thanksgiving and Christmas at my house, my three brothers trooping in with their girlfriends, later kids and wives, me in the kitchen wrestling a big pimply turkey around, pouring coffee, washing dishes, shooing the dogs and cats away from the table, then falling exhausted onto the camp mattress I'd thrown onto the uncarpeted floor. All this, I've come to realize, I could do in a rented house as well.

But I don't really want to rent a house again. I've grown to appreciate the freedom in calling a place mine. No landlords. No rules. Yet I found I don't love my house as much as the houses of my childhood. Perhaps I've already started to wrap them in the gauzy aura of nostalgia; my childhood houses are the repositories of my childhood memories. Then again, in those days I had the luxury of innocence. My parents were there to care for my well-being, my brothers were there to torment and laugh with. I wasn't the one who counted the endless procession of mortgage payments, roof repairs, and taxes. With both my parents dead, with that last line of defense against my own mortality gone, I'm the one now who sees the line of mortgage payments stretching out like the beckoning monotony of the highway's yellow lines.

It's not as if I haven't grown fond of my house. I love the upstairs bathroom, a converted sunporch with a built-in daybed, and my bedroom-study feels like the homiest place in the world on a rainy day. But despite it's well-worn charm it needs a lot of care. The floors need refinishing, the basement is damp and leaky when it rains, and the kitchen hasn't been updated since the house was built in 1910. I worry that it will soon need a new roof, a furnace; I'll have to borrow money and put myself deeper in debt. When I bought the house I had some vague notions that I'd like to tinker and fix, but now I seldom want to be bothered, except in the spring when I go through a frenzy of yard work and sprucing up. I work and teach and write and do aerobics and ski and travel. I just don't have time to reglaze that window or rebuild that front step.

If you really cared, you'd make time, you'd rearrange your priorities, my nagging, responsible inner voice pipes up. That's precisely what I have to admit to myself. I don't care enough about this house to make its upkeep my priority. I actually resent having to put money into the house. Would I rather refinish the downstairs floors or laze away an afternoon drinking café au lait in the French Quarter? Waterproof the basement or mountain bike through the rugged forests of northern Minnesota? Paint the house or sea kayak in Glacier Bay? No contest. Instead of counting sheep to fall asleep at night I imagine I'm an adventure travel writer for *Outside* magazine. Where to go next? Patagonia? Irian Jaya? Antarctica? Machu Picchu?

Every weekend my neighbors up and down the block are out fixing things or building things or planting things. In winter they bustle into their houses on Saturday mornings with lumber, or large sacks from WalMart or Menards. Their houses seem to be their sole preoccupation outside of their jobs. The retired couple across the street have matching snowblowers, matching lawnmowers, and, I've heard from the paper boy, matching recliners with separate TVs. They have a large boat and massive RV parked behind their house, but I've never seen them go anywhere. Instead they appear to spend all the clement months outside on lawn patrol, carefully planting plastic flowers and peering at the comings and goings of the three lesbian households in our block. Around the neighborhood I have the uneasy sense that home improvement is a competition I'm somehow losing. Even Sarah and Kate next door spend all their free time in the garden or working on their house. I smile and wave as I carry my mountain bike or ski bag out to the Jeep, then nervously glance at the front of the house to make sure that at least I managed to drag the garbage off the front porch. Some days, walking up the street on my way home from work, I look at my house and it makes me feel tired, burdened; other days I can barely wait to get inside where it's comfortable, where I feel at home. I guess I have the kind of ambivalent relationship with my house that I had with a scratchy old woolen sweater I had in college: despite its itchy ugliness it kept me warm, it smelled like me, I could always count on it, and it was mine.

Everyone from my friends to *Consumer Reports* tells me that owning my home is the smartest financial move I can make. It's an investment, a tax shelter, a savings account. I feel guilty that I'm not happier with the new bathroom floor and toilet, that I'm not excited about the new storm windows I had installed. Sometimes I think I'm a failure at being a homeowner. Maybe I'd learn to love another house better, I try to console myself, one that needed less care. I flirt with the idea of moving to the country, flip through the real estate supplements for acreages and land. No nosy, competitive neighbors, and all that space, all that nature. Or maybe I'd like this house better if I paid to have the floors refinished, the kitchen remodeled, got furniture that wasn't cat-clawed thrift shop. Marked it more and more as mine. Or maybe that's part of the problem. Would I feel differently if "mine" were truly an "ours"? If I had someone to share the worries and repairs? Maybe I simply haven't lived here long enough for the house to have soaked up enough memories to give it the heft of *place* that my childhood homes carry. Looking back I think that buying the house was a way of coping with my mother's death, though I didn't see it at the time. My way of saying, Hey, we'll be okay. I'm an adult; I bought a house; my brothers and I still have a home.

In the long list of instructions my mother left after the doctors told her to put her affairs in order, among notes about legal affairs, her car's water pump problems, and how to get the hard water stains off the crystal, she wrote personal notes to us as they occurred to her. One was: "After I die you will all feel a sense of inner assurance and capability that comes only after the death of both parents. This is very freeing. Utilize it as a strength." Thinking of these words as I drive down the eternal ribbon of August highway, I start to realize I don't need to prove my responsibility, I don't need to stay in the house or the city simply for the sake of staying, as if stability and home owner-ship were a virtue in its own right. Taking a deep breath, I smile as I aim for the far horizon.

～～

Well, not exactly. Though I wanted to keep driving, I really aimed for Iowa City, and home after a trying weekend watching over my brother in an intensive care ward in Glenview, Illinois. Two years after our mother died, my youngest brother Ben was diagnosed with Hodgkin's lymphoma. Now, after the rounds of chemo and radia-tion, his doctors believed he'd beaten the cancer, but he'd become critically ill with pneumocystis, a virulent form of pneumonia. I'd just come back from three weeks in the Alaskan wilderness and it had shocked me to see how sick Ben was, to sit amid the hiss and pump of oxygen machines and watch him struggle for air. As I watched the monitor where a flash of numbers charted his blood oxygen level, I thought of what Ben had gone though in his thirty years: father dead of a sudden heart attack when he was twelve, mother dead from a potently effective cancer two years earlier, his own year-long battle with cancer, and now this.

"I just want my life back," Ben said. I knew he was utterly worn down, demoralized. I watched the nurses sit him up and force air into his lungs, watched them poke more lines into his veins, give him a blood transfusion. I told him stories about Alaska, made jokes, went home and scrubbed his apartment, bought groceries and stocked his cupboards. His girlfriend teased him and held his hand. Three days later he said he had a chance for season tickets for the Cubs the next summer, and maybe he'd take them. I knew he'd recovered enough for me to leave.

Driving back to Iowa City, I thought that as much as buying a house was a response to my mother's death, so was my trip to Alaska, my fantasies of life on the road, my yearning to travel. Mulling over the words she had written, I discovered that maybe I'd misunderstood what that freedom she'd talked about meant. Early on, I'd thought that my buying a house was a sign of my "inner assurance" and "capability." I'd wanted to provide that staple of the traditional American narrative: a stable, fixed base for my brothers and me, a home. Yet after these few years of lukewarm ownership I'd also come to realize that it's not the house—the physical structure—that matters. This most recent Thanksgiving our whole tiny clan gathered at my brother Pete's one bedroom apartment, slept on the floor, and had a wonderful time.

As I stared at the campers and trailers rumbling by, I wondered if what she really meant was that we should use our freedom as an opportunity. Seeing Ben so gaunt and ill brought back the refrain, clichéd but true, that had echoed in me since my father and mother had died: Life's too short not to do what your heart tells you.

"But how do you know what's the right thing to do?" Ben asks me ten months after his bout of pneumonia, as we sit in my kitchen on a rainy spring day. Now that he's healthy he's trying to sort out the rest of his life. We used to tease Ben about being born acting like a forty year old. He was reading *Time* cover to cover at six. At seven he had business cards printed. At ten he asked for *krugerands* for Christmas. He's marched through his life sure of himself, sure of his choices. Until now. Now he's not sure he wants to stay with his job teaching high school, not sure he wants to stay in Chicago, not sure he wants to stay with his girlfriend. For the past several years, he's been dogged by the idea of going to seminary to study for the priesthood. Looking at him across the table I think he's been stunned into a new relationship with his life, the very frailness of his body at once a betrayal and a license, a permission. And like me, the lesson he's walked away with, unsure how to use it, is this freedom to make his life anything he chooses.

It's the choosing that's the hard part. I recently found a picture taken when I was not quite four. I'm riding my Wonder Horse in front of the TV, wearing a white shirt and corduroys, cowboy boots and a kerchief. I've got a rope lassoed around my waist. Beneath the horse are a Mickey Mouse guitar and a set of Mickey Mouse ears. After Gene Autry or Roy Rogers came the Mickey Mouse Club, and with a quick change I'd become a Mouseketeer, singing and strumming along with Annette and Bobby. As easy as that.

"Not a day goes by that I don't wish my life were different," I tell Ben, and it's true. Even though I have a job I like, friends, the house, and animals to care for, I seem obsessed with reimagining my life. "Here's what I've thought of in the past few weeks," I say. "I'm going to quit my job and move to Grand Marais on Lake Superior, or find a cabin back in the woods, be a bartender at the local tavern, and write. I'm going to move to Alaska and learn to fly an airplane, be a bush pilot and raise sled dogs. I'm going to move to Ireland and work as a stable hand and become an activist. After reading Gretel Ehrlich and Jim Galvin I want to move out to Wyoming or Montana, get a trailer at the edge of the mountains, bartend and write in some kick-dirt little town. Or, when I rein myself in, I'm going to sell my house and move out to the country on at least thirty-five acres with woods and a creek, become the Annie Dillard of Iowa."

"Wow," Ben says, "maybe it's genetic." I can tell he feels better.

I suspect most people fantasize about alternative lives, but I realized that most of my lives involve moving somewhere else— alone. Just as I'd bought into the narrative of owning a house, I'd also internalized the narrative of the "couple" as the mature lesbian way of life. Until I broke up with Myra, I'd had one relationship after another since I was sixteen, with never more than a couple of months in between. And after a year of living together as roommates after we broke up I realized I needed to break the habit of my reliance on her for built-in companionship. We both saw that we weren't extending ourselves out of the comfortable range of our mutual patterns. When I asked, she agreed that it would be best for both of us if she moved out.

"I guess I'm a slow learner," I say to Ben. "And maybe I was always afraid. I think I needed the mirror of someone else to show me who I am. Now I need to see who I am by myself for a while." It's ironic, I think to myself, how only after the death of both our parents do Ben and I feel we can make such life-altering changes. Ben's likely to leave his tenure level teaching job to go back to college to study for the priesthood, and I'm just now realizing I don't have to accept the narratives I thought I always wanted or needed in order to feel responsible. Maybe this is what our mother meant all along.

"You know what I really want sometimes," I tell Ben, "is to be free. Free to go anywhere I want, with enough money to do it the way I want to, with a new Jeep and an Airstream." I imagine already how cozy I'd be, puttering at the stove, stepping over the dog curled on the tiny braided rug, or watching the news on the tiny TV while I ate, then stepping out to stretch and yawn under the star-shot western sky. I'd be alone but not lonely, mobile and self-contained. At home as I headed for the far horizon.

TERRY WOLVERTON

~℮~

A Community of the Imagination

It doesn't look like anyone's idea of home. The faded blue walls are bare of art or any adornment. The squat, windowless room lacks architectural grace. A beige paneled ceiling is routinely disrupted by banks of fluorescent lights. Mottled green industrial carpet covers not only the floor but creeps up all four walls to waist height, meant to protect the vertical surfaces from wear.

That strategy hasn't worked. The walls are smudged by hand-prints and haloes of hair grease left by anonymous lolling. Gray metal folding chairs line the wall like sentinels. The folding tables are mismatched—some wood grain, some flat gray, others a lighter heathered gray reminiscent of linoleum. The veneer peels up on a few, others bear dents or gouges in their corners, and all are topped with a sticky layer of cola and spilled coffee that can never seem to be scrubbed away.

You're getting the picture: a worn room in an institutional setting, in this case the Gay & Lesbian Center in Los Angeles. It's a room occupied by hundreds of people every week: the recovering addict at the Saturday morning meeting of Marijuana Anonymous; the quietly hopeful young man sitting through the workshop on "New Treatments for AIDS"; the underpaid and over-caffeinated program staffer with a five o'clock grant deadline; the newly out lesbian at a rap group looking for the woman of her dreams.

For these people the room is a way-station, a quick stop on their journey to someplace else. But, undecorated and heavily trafficked as it is, Room 111 has been a kind of home to the participants in the Perspectives Writing Program, which I founded at the Center in 1988. Over a hundred people each year have attended one of four free weekly workshops; most have found support to make a home inside their own creativity, and a community within these four unspectacular walls.

It's a program designed primarily for lesbians and gay men, but it's also utilized by bisexuals, transgendered people, and even a few heterosexuals who pull me aside to ask privately if it's all right for them to be there. Appreciation of diversity is one of the values that undergirds the program. The pierced and tattooed twenty-three-year-old performance artist exchanges feedback with the fifty-five-year-old gay father who's writing his memoirs. The *veterana* from

East L.A. trades jokes with the African-American army reservist. The male-to-female transgender gives make-up tips to a shy lesbian.

Feeling at home inside our creativity is a challenge for most of us. We don't live in a society that prizes the imagination, the vocation of the artist. We are not taught that creativity is our birthright; we are told to behave, to conform, to hide, to be silent. We are taught that the world will be at best indifferent, at worst hostile to our expression.

For those of us further marginalized as women, lesbians, gay men, transgendered, people of color, blue collar, and/or people battered or sexually abused as children, the oppression of our creative selves becomes insidiously fused with the oppressions of race, class, gender and sexual orientation. If our very lives are seen to have no value, we reason, of what possible importance could be our art?

There's so much to be reclaimed: the imagination retrieved from its burial ground of fear; one's voice raised again after years of muteness; a vision restored of oneself as someone who matters, whose stories have meaning for others. This work cannot be done in isolation. It requires support and feedback; it requires the healing presence of community. This reclamation is part of the mission of the Perspectives Program.

When participants come to the program they expect to be given assignments, to be taught some techniques, to receive feedback on their efforts. These things do occur.

What they don't expect is to find community among people markedly different from themselves, whose only similarity may be a passion for words, some stories that urgently need to be told, a desire to make their voices heard. If the physical surroundings of Room 111 provide an unlikely home, the workshop participants come to comprise a most unexpected family.

~~

Let me tell you what kind of girl I am: in my personal lexicon, *home* is a four-letter word. By any conventional definition—the place of one's upbringing, the abode of one's family of origin, one's private domicile or the scene of blissful cohabitation—the word is a vulgarity to me. I see it this way: home is a place to escape from, to leave behind, to erase all traces of.

I'm the one who, at age five, announced that I would never marry, never have children. Who, after declaring myself an atheist at age nine, kept on going to church because it was the only way to get out of my parents' house on Sundays. Who, at age eleven, dreamed of growing up to live in the John Hancock Tower in Chicago, an environment as public and impersonal as I could imagine.

I'm the one who spent years "sleeping over" at the homes and apartments of my lovers, who kept changes of clothes in the trunk of my car, who visited my own bungalow only to pick up the mail. The one who lived for four years with a broken refrigerator and didn't feel inconvenienced. Who, in the days when I had a regular job, routinely went to the office on holidays: Christmas Eve, Fourth of July, Labor Day. To my coworkers I explained that I could "get more done when it's quiet"; how could I let them know that home was most toxic on so-called special occasions?

I'm the one who, when I finally lived with my lover in a home we bought together, would be lighthearted and amorous whenever we were away from home—on a date, an outing, a vacation—but would freeze up, tight and hollow, melancholy, as our car pulled into our driveway. The one who, alone now in my rented house, feels most comfortable in my office, the other rooms unfurnished, still clogged with boxes.

It's not that I hunger to be rootless, without a stable base on which to rest. It is rather that what appears solid has proven to be quicksand, the firm foundation dissolving to dust. Perhaps it's no accident that I migrated from the midwest to southern California, where the very ground shifts and shudders beneath my feet.

⁓

Home is, after all, the site of family. In theory, a place of safety. When it is instead a place where a child is awakened by yelling, where baked potatoes and pans of dishwater are hurled as weapons, where people are chased with knives, where gunshots are fired in the kitchen, where a stepfather masturbates into a five-year-old's reluctantly held out palm, where every ritual—from getting up in the morning to dinner-time—is lubricated with gin, there is no safety at home.

Home, the site of family. In theory, a place of belonging. Being a misfit in one's family of origin—the only one sober when every-body's drunk, the only one who reads while others pass out in front of the TV, the lesbian among heterosexuals, the grown-up child among childish adults, the one who still dreams when everyone else has given up—makes it impossible to belong at home. Either the misfit is cast out, made scapegoat and sent into exile, or is expected to sever pieces of self in order to fit the slot that's been made for her.

I survived my childhood home with four primary strategies:

I sought my sense of identity outside my home, at school. In school I worked hard and got good grades and lots of validation for it. I took on extra assignments and participated in every extracur-ricular activity they offered, from service squad to glee club, from art classes to roles in the school play. I began to see myself as somone who *did* things, and it not only rewarded me with positive feedback, but also relieved the boredom of the unrelenting drama of home.

I formed primary bonds with my friends, who became in my mind a kind of substitute family. I wanted to see Marilyn every day, wanted to talk on the phone to her late at night, often to the irrita-tion of her parents. I wanted Patty to be available on Sundays, holi-days, all those family times. And if Denise and I fought, I would pester her with phone calls and notes passed in math class until she relented; I couldn't bear to have her mad at me. I was a leader who was desperately dependent on my followers; the friendships were always more important to me than they were to Marilyn or Patty or Denise, they who had safer homes, who felt less dissonant with their blood relations.

Although mine was not a cultured family—my parents worked at jobs they hated, drank, and fell asleep in front of the tube—my mother encouraged me to read and I did so ceaselessly. During summers I could read a book a day. Books allowed me to experience (and therefore envision) realities other than my own; reading both fed my imagination and fueled my desire for escape.

Most importantly, I wrote. I understood early that the power of words was the gift of meaning. The poetry and stories I wrote then allowed me to define my own identity on the page, gave me something to do with the pain I felt, and allowed me to transform life through my imagination, to transport myself into a different meaning.

I was restless after high school. I enrolled in and dropped out of three different colleges in Detroit, Toronto, and Grand Rapids, Michigan. I was waitressing to earn a living. I wanted to be an actress, an artist, a writer, but those circles seemed dominated by men who could not see me except as potential sex partner. I was a feminist, a lesbian, but I didn't want to wear flannel shirts and give up lipstick; didn't want to subsume art for politics.

Eventually my seeking led me across the continent to join the community of writers, artists, and performers at the Woman's Building in Los Angeles. It was here I learned that art need not be a solitary pursuit, that creativity can thrive in a climate of support, encouragement, and constructive criticism. I spent thirteen years working in this environment, which nurtured my art, encouraged my ambition, delighted in my achievements, and supported me to risk further. You could say it was my home.

And although the Woman's Building shut its doors, dissolving as have so many other homes, my sojourn there gave me the vision and skills of community building, the tools to create my home in the world.

～

Community. It's a problematic word, makes thinking people nervous. We fear that the assumption of commonality will blot out difference, cultural particularity, individuality. That the establishment of a "women's community" or "gay community" too often dictates a monolithic stance that negates the distinctions of class, race, and personal preference. That the cost of belonging is surrender of opposing points of view. We're so nervous about being swallowed up that we can scarcely imagine a setting in which our individual voices might be respected, our differences observed and appreciated without being judged, our efforts applauded, our progress exclaimed.

On the first day of class I talk to my students, tell them that this community is within their reach, that it is an integral part of my vision for the writing program. If they are new students, this information has little meaning for them. They huddle in their folding chairs, viewing the other students—strangers in this moment—with suspicion: are they better writers than I am or worse? are they going to be weirdos? will I ever like any of them? will any of them like me? They distrust my promise of community, yet they hunger for it. I've asked them, "Do you know other writers with whom you can discuss your work or your writing process?" and most have answered, "No."

At the beginning of each class session we go around the room, and the students are asked to talk about how their writing has gone in the past week, what inspired them, what they've produced, what obstacles got in their way, what issues they've wrestled with, what they've learned from wrestling. A lot of people cringe at this part of the process; they don't like to speak up in class, hate having to report on themselves. Still, it's important that all get to acknowledge themselves as writers in front of the others. And when one says, "I make time to write but then I find myself cleaning the refrigerator instead," and another suggests, "Why don't we make a writing date and get together so we can both stay on track?" they've not only formed a bond around that particular problem, but have begun to see their classmates as potential resources for support and solutions.

The exercises I assign in class are designed to encourage surprise and risk, a playfulness without which the imagination will not thrive. I want my students to try things they've never done before, I want them to make mistakes. I tell them, "You must write badly in order to write well." I insist that it is the job of a first draft to be bad, and encourage them to not be in too great a hurry to achieve a finished product. I want to help them feel safe within their imaginations, to explore unknown territory; to free them from the dictates of the inner critic, the impossible pressure to be perfect. I want to help them make a home inside their creativity, a place for the self to reside.

Time is also made in class for students to read what they've written. This is always voluntary; there's no forced exposure. We read not for critical feedback but for what we call "the witness function," so that others observe and acknowledge that one has written. Pat A. reads about her *loca* homegirls; Robert reveals the sad isolation of privilege; Sheila rocks us with a tale about seducing the minister's wife. We take delight in each other's stories. The student who's convinced that his or her writing is worthless suddenly sees interest in the faces of classmates; the possibility dawns: this might be meaningful to someone else.

Usually after a few weeks someone will take the step to bring the group together outside of the workshop, going out for coffee or a meal after class, coming together for a writing date to accomplish the assigned homework, attending a reading together. It is in these gatherings that the students disclose the personal details of their lives, share the stories that have yet to make it onto paper, or the stories behind the stories that they've written. Lasting friendships develop as part of this process, one-on-one and in small groups, and students begin to feel the tentative beginnings of community.

This isn't to suggest that we've achieved utopia. Because it is a creative writing program I insist on the freedom of expression, and sometimes misunderstandings or hurt feelings result. A man writes about a girl being molested by her father, and a woman in the class has her own memories triggered. A woman makes a thoughtless jab at men in general and is accused of male-bashing. A white student inquires about why there needs to be a Black History Month. A bisexual woman reminds us that the umbrella of "gay and lesbian" does not shelter her. The diversity of backgrounds and experience within the program is a challenge to our ignorance, prejudice and solipsism, and these challenges require courage, and honest negotiation. Preserving the balance between cultural sensitivity and freedom of expression is a delicate operation, but as writers, what other stance can we responsibly take?

Twice during the eleven-month classes, we hold potluck parties. There are two requirements: bring food to share with your classmates, and bring something that you've written to read aloud to them. We savor the chance to try Jean's eggrolls, Pat A.'s homemade *salcita,* David's fava beans, Ana's brownies, and we also thrill to the stories let loose in the room, cheering what each writer has accomplished.

At the end of each year the students give a reading of their work for the public. Many of them approach the process with great trepidation, convinced that they'll die of fright, that they'll falter and be unable to make it through. We spend the weeks leading up to the reading in preparation: choosing their selections and editing them for the time limit; learning to make eye contact and project the voice; practicing, practicing, practicing. Often students will get together in small groups to rehearse, giving each other encouragement and feedback on reading techniques. When the day of the reading arrives, every student does a magnificent job, and all of them are as thrilled and delighted for their fellow students' successes as for their own. When the workshop is over, they can scarcely bear to part. "It's my village," declares Pat B., and he speaks for all of us.

~

I spend most of my weeknights and all day Saturday teaching workshops in the writing program. My lovers and cats have protested my lack of available time but I'm unswayed. I am drawn to that faded blue room, the banged-up folding tables and uncomfortable chairs, as I imagine some early ancestor drawn to the warmth of a firelit cave against the cold darkness.

"You give so much," my students say, admiring. "You give too much," my friends and lovers say, with resentment. What neither group understands is what I get back, my own creativity nurtured. When David shares the astonishing new story he's written, when Ana overcomes her resistance to poetic form and writes a sonnet that is published, when Georgia reads in front of an audience for the first time, there's a little more room in the world for my own voice and vision.

If where I feel safest is in front of sheets of paper with a pen in my hand, if where I belong is not to a biological group or a political category but to a group of people engaged in artistic endeavor, if my home is not a plot of ground, not walls and a roof but the limitless chambers of my imagination, then why wouldn't these workshop participants become my family?

Those less charitable have said that my ego must be in sorry shape to see my students as my community. "Pathetic," I can hear them thinking, "the need to retain that power, that sense of superiority. She couldn't hack it with her peers. She ought to get a life." But in terms of ability and skills, if not in longevity or credentials, a number of my students are already my peers and others are on their way to becoming so. I see us engaged in the same pursuit: to reclaim that spark that burns inside us, to nurture it into a strong clean flame, to find the courage to let loose that light into the world. I have been farther down the trail than some of them, overcome certain pitfalls, and been carefully observant of the landscape; this qualifies me to serve as leader of the expedition, but we are all traveling the same path.

This is not to say that I don't recognize differences between us. When I first started teaching, back in the '70s when we were suspicious of all hierarchies of power, I was eager to erase any separation between myself and my students. Over time I learned that this stance was about my own discomfort with leadership and responsibility, and that it was not honest. What I came to understand was that most students need that sense of separation, need to see me as someone who is not in the same place as they are, need to have a model to which to aspire. I don't try to maintain a mystique; I am very candid with my classes about my own writing process, I dutifully report my blocks and rejections and disappointments along with my ambitions and successes. If I'm wrestling with a writing problem, I talk about it, along with any solution I might have hit upon. Sometimes my students suggest solutions, and I'm grateful for them. As a working writer, I can demonstrate what that life is like, the roadblocks as well as the moments of joy, the slow progress toward a destination that is never reached.

There's a price to pay for being this role of the teacher: no matter how close I come to my students there is always a slight remove. I can't be one of the gang, just another participant. This is one of the ironies of what I do: out of my own need for belonging, I've created a community for which I am the source and to which I can never entirely belong. Reading a draft of this essay, my friend Lynette insightfully observes, "You're the mother and the child." It's true, my need for this home is no less great than for any of the students who find respite there.

And a final irony, this one pointed out by Sally: "A good mother raises her kids to leave," as of course, a good teacher does as well.

~

Between the time I conceptualized this essay and my actual writing of it, I lost my home. I mean, my address, the place where I slept at night and where my clothes nestled in a closet. My lover of nine years announced that she was attracted to someone new, that she could "no longer access her desire for me."

I don't know why I was surprised. I know this happens every day: commitments are erased, bonds are dissolved, once-solid ground shifts like sand. Having worked to set down roots with someone, in some place, I thought the spell would be powerful enough to hold.

The house I had loved, the garden I'd tended was no longer a place of safety, had ceased to be somewhere I belonged.

It was the women and men of my writing community, my students, who helped me through the transition. David and Eitan took me to dinner and listened as I wailed. Ellen loaned me a refrigerator, Yvonne gave me a stove. Kathy installed phone jacks. Elise spent hours one hot August afternoon assembling bookcases. Mary Cecille came with her truck and her dolly to move the appliances, and Megan helped her. Sue transported another loaned bookcase across town in her truck. A whole army of them came and packed car- and truckloads of my belongings and moved them to my rented house. Kathryn smudged the new place with sage. Ana took me to Ikea to buy a chest of drawers and loaned me a TV.

Without them I would have felt wretched and exiled. And though I am broken-hearted, I am not destitute. I have family. I am safe. I belong.

~

I don't have a couch or comfortable chairs. I don't have a washer and dryer or a stereo system and my living room is still clogged with boxes. But this month I opened the doors to a new writing center in Los Angeles, a space called Writers at Work.

My nine-year residency at the Gay & Lesbian Center ended this summer, just as my nine-year relationship with my lover was coming apart. I was determined to keep my community together, and so I have rented a space for our workshops to continue.

The walls are painted a bright creamy yellow. There are lush plants in the windows, large windows that look out onto sky and trees. There are still folding tables, but they are new, matching, and not yet crusty; the folding chairs have padding on the seats and backs.

Only writers will use this room and so we have a small reference library with dictionary and thesaurus, lots of back issues of literary magazines, a subscription to *Poets & Writers*. We have our own (leased) photocopier, and in a few weeks we will have our own (used) computer.

The space is a gift to myself and to my community, and already it gives back. Hilary donates electrical work. Michael does all the painting. Mark supervises the procurement and installation of carpet and miniblinds. Georgia mails flyers and brochures. Pat and Mary-Linn contribute shelving. Elise and Celeste donate an old refrigerator. Kathy and Erin and Sally and Mary and David and Eitan and George and Eileen and Carolyn and Kharon and Ana and Pat and Megan and Jim spend an entire Saturday assembling furniture, cleaning, and getting the space in shape. Thom organizes the party for the open house. Seventy-plus people attend and celebrate.

I can barely wait to see what will take root here, in our new home.

M. PAZ GALUPO

~e~

Between Two Tongues

My lover loves me in two different languages. She tells me this with her mouth on mine so I can feel the difference. In English, her love fills my mouth; her tongue meets mine, slaps at it playfully (I love you). In Spanish, she breathes her love in and out of me, steals some of my breath before completely covering my lips with hers (*Te amo*). I imagine myself loved twice over. Loved more deeply because she allows her two worlds to intersect somewhere between her mouth and mine.

My father, my aunts, refused to speak anything but English to me as a child. They didn't want me to have to understand what it's like to be different. My father, after twenty-nine years in the States, is subconsciously American. He dreams at night of convertible sports cars, of peanut butter and Tab, of high-risk investments. His dreams are scripted in perfect English and acted out against a backdrop of four distinct seasons. Despite everyone's best intentions, I haven't escaped an understanding of difference. I understand that twenty-nine years didn't cut deep enough into my father's thick Filipino accent, didn't lighten his skin or make him any less a target (subconscious not-withstanding). Twenty-nine years still finds my father a foreigner in a country that he claims (without regret) as his home.

A childhood of English taught me that difference is provoking and offensive. Taught me that my father's jagged accent interrupts the flow of polite conversation and offends the American ear. It offends the ear of an American man at the gas station on a Saturday afternoon. My father explains this to me when he returns home adjusting the neck of his shirt, smoothing the wrinkles in his dress pants with the sweat from his palms. My understanding of difference, however, extends beyond my father. It extends beyond myself in every direction as I walk down the street with my lover. For each situation, I understand the need to identify the line where difference inspires hatred. Where my love for a woman could easily turn to violence used against her. Where my lover's sweet whisper fills my mouth with broken glass and broken teeth.

My lover wears her hair long. I tell my aunts about her, about her long dark hair that reminds me of theirs. They don't understand when I tell them that her hair falls thick down her back. That I get lost each time my fingers brush through it, weaving her hair into my own. They don't recognize anything familiar in the excited tone of my voice. The idea of romantic love and marriage is lost on my immigrant family. My aunts have long abandoned the notion of love, traded it in for U.S. citizenship. They marry men twenty years their senior in hasty ceremonies and motorcycle honeymoons. They throw their wedding vows across metal folding chairs in a living room too small to contain the usual culinary aromas: pancit, steamed rice, *bico, sampañya* (blood pudding). Their sacrifice becomes clear in the lazy reflection of plastic wrap stretched tightly over wedding-day leftovers. My aunts left the Philippines, their families, their own children, their home, to live in trailer parks and dirt worm farms in rural Ohio.

I fight to keep myself from passing judgement against my aunts. They've made their sacrifice that affords them the ability to redefine themselves in a culture that only blames them for their difference. And when they return to the Philippines, for a funeral or a visit, they are blamed just as viciously. They are blamed for the death of their parents, for abandoning the rest of the family, for being traitors to their culture. In redefining themselves, my father and my aunts necessarily separated themselves from all they had known. From most of what is. They've had to create a vulnerable space for them-selves. And they had to exist in it, to call it home.

Whether my family understands it or not, their sacrifice has everything to do with the way I enjoy my lover's long hair. It has everything to do with the luxury I now have to reach across cultures and reclaim the notion of romantic love. I reclaim it for my aunts (though they would deny having anything to do with my love for a woman). I reclaim it for myself.

My family doesn't understand why I want to marry my lover. They don't understand my desire to stomp on fresh cut flowers, press wedding cake between my fingers, spray champagne into the air. I want to stand before my aunts, their aged husbands. I want to stand visible and vulnerable, in my black boots and my tube socks. I want to declare my sincere intent to follow the silver band around my lover's finger. *Ahora y siempre.* Til death do us part. On cue my lover will kiss me. One kiss, in two different languages so that no one mistakes the love between us. My fingers will braid the long strands of her hair into mine. My tongue will rest at home in her mouth.

LINDA SMUKLER

~e~

The Color of Home

1. East Hill Road

Walk outside the door into the cool morning   let the animals out   ten minutes later call to them to make sure they are safe home is safe the world is safe as I am safe walking out into the day as safe as the spirit in my head has decided I will be   I call and comfort myself that my animals still walk the earth that the streams of cars and raccoons and foxes and coyotes   coyotes especially   don't carry them off like once happened to my Mikey who I thought it was my job to protect   I tried hard but not hard enough because one day I called and she did not come at first not so unusual but for the gray cast in the sky the fight I had with my lover the unsettled quiver in my belly the empty air that greeted her name   for two days I called   three   then four   I heard screams in the night and still could not save her even when I ran out into the dark air to follow the sound through the dense wall of woods surrounding the house   nothing answered my call except my own expectation my will my supreme desire except my own failure against Mikey's wild life   her venture forth   a plan bigger than her knowledge or my own   except a love too big to bear without an answer

2. Mallory Road (The Blessing)

You pull up in a borrowed BMW   your face soft   red-cheeked   you smell faintly of chlorine   a clean sweat smell   delicate and bathed dressed in cotton and silk   smooth under my hands   we circle the house soon to be but not yet ours   we peer in windows   hover around perimeters   the land a bowl which we bless   driveway   birch tree   willow   woodpile   swamp   we follow no rule   risk exposure without modesty or circumspection   we maintain no sense of decency in this rural life where even under the cover of night you tell me not to start   but where I have already begun I cannot stop compelled to take you naked in a leather seat   windows open unwilling to hide our cries   our benediction

3. Mallory Road

The color of home a smooth yellow cup handed to me by you with strong-wristed competence   tea to wake me on this sunny late-

winter morning   the color of home a dirty green couch whose bulk
and heaviness we fight with a lavender-blue sheet   the color of
home air and white   a backdrop for reds and the sable of our dog
the smudge grey of one cat and the tawny gold of the other   the
color of home a red rooster mask and a copper wedding jug on the
tall stone mantle   the orange of my computer screen emblazoned
with highlights of purple and gold   the mustard ochre we once
thought we'd paint the house   a drawer of white t-shirts   my blue
bottle in the sun   pale pink tiles in the bathroom   the beam above
a dark green   the color of home a little toy duck a blue horse a
Mexican fish a ceramic Christmas cactus with red dots for blossoms
and improbable bluebirds in the branches   the oatmeal grey flannel
of your pajamas surrounding your body in the red chair   a red dust
pan on the slate blue floor

4. Mallory Road (The Ocean at the Bottom of the Road)

You run into the house and yell Come look Sam! Come! There's an
ocean at the bottom of the road!   You're kidding I say   you grab my
arm and pull me from my desk   No you say   I'm serious   I got down
there and you know the cow field?   Which cow field? I ask   The one
at the bottom of the road   It's not there anymore   There's no more
barn no more farmhouse no more road   I don't believe you I say   you
drag me out the door and the dog follows   it's early August   sun high

tomatoes trying to get ripe   one of the most beautiful days of the summer   I've walked out this door with you every morning but today I immediately notice that something has indeed changed   there's a salt breeze in the air and you have a strange energy about you   excited and driven   your body propels me forward   we run and the dog runs with us   we get half-way down the dirt road when you touch the inside of my arm   There!   Look!   I do look and I see our world suddenly stopped at a body of water so huge I cannot make out the other side where is the farmhouse?   the barn the field the cows?   I thought we had gone to a party last night   that we danced for the first time in all our years together   that we had come home   tried to watch a movie and fell asleep   the kittens chased our feet under the quilt and they were certainly still kittens this morning   but look   there is the ocean as clear as day   we race down to the edge of the water and marvel   it is as if the entire county has become a bowl and we are standing on an island inside   what will become of us?   I do understand that our life will completely change   will we become fishermen?   explorers?   it has been hard these years to figure out time and money to transport ourselves elsewhere   now the ocean has finally come to take us

5. Arizona

One morning I woke up it was green and the next morning I woke up it was brown   one morning I looked outside there was the blue

spruce I always wished for when I was a child because I thought it
was a tree so perfect so firm and blue and then an umbrella of catalpa
leaves a wall of weeds and maple and oak blocking Gordon's house
across the road   a wood thrush robins and chickadees   *ptuu ptui*
then one morning I woke up and it was brown and the earth was
dusty with one small cactus no longer in April bloom another with
fish hooks and next to it a light gray cottonwood   only a hint of pale
green after a so-called monsoon   one morning I woke up and it was
brown but there was a sky and mountains that turned red at night
holding me in a landscape I had never known   one morning I woke
up sweating because I did not have a job but I looked up and saw
bright blue from Mexico and some orange too and even my dog had
a tan and I thought I am at home here thawing out from fear and
forty-two winters and there you were too in the bed next to me and
I love you now dressed in yellow and Hank called to say come sit in
my earth house and lean into the purple brown walls

6. South Fifth Avenue

At the end of a journey a yellow wall   a bit of heat but not so bad
a breeze that shakes the cottonwood leaves   a purple flower   the
king Max on his stairs   at the end of a journey your mouth on my
belly   dogs bark next door   Babka's heavy weight against my thigh
one cat chews my head while another jumps out the screen   the

early sun and the field down the street   *Should we get up?   Will the heat be too bad in an hour?   It's Monday*   you insistent through all of it   bringing me slow and close then far away again   now the keyboard under my fingers   one cricket or more   at the end of a journey the desert or the savannah and it isn't really silence but wind and a coffee cup while Max runs across his yard after lizards   a few birds   Smudge rests in the open door of her kitchen   at the end of a journey our neighborhood our street no longer *road*   the ice cream truck drives up with its little tune and you buy me a cherry banana in lieu of root beer and then the rains   storms at the end of a journey where our animals already protect the boundaries of their home   no more boxes to unpack or maybe just one that keeps giving back gifts I turn on the TV bang on the piano stomp on the wood floor all rhythms mine   booming like the thunder outside a monsoon not of my making but the loud voice of god

❧

As The Roots of the Trees

"The Plains States are the heart of our nation, and that heart beats slow and sure…"

—TIME-LIFE LIBRARY OF AMERICA

A boy, maybe twelve, in a T-shirt and baggy jeans, is down on his knees, wrists pinned behind his back with plastic handcuffs. Two policemen on huge-rumped horses flank him. As I leave my downtown Minneapolis hotel, six or seven police cars arrive, racing up the sidewalks. So many raging sirens over one small kid. The boy looks resigned to his fate, an innocent in some religious icon painting—head bent and body kneeling. What was his sin?

It's an introduction, of some kind, to the contradictions of the Midwest.

❧

I walk ahead to the Black Forest Inn and meet Sally. Crowded, the outdoor patio sounds like lunchtime in a cafeteria: relaxed, loud, daily. Sweating, showy heterosexuals celebrate the June weather with mugs of German beer.

We get a table, and I lean back and look around. Traveling always feels like doing drugs. Blink and the world changes: the temperature, the faces, the color of the sky. Today it's Minneapolis; tomorrow the green fields of Iowa, and then onwards to the Nebraska plains and the dry Dakotas. I've finally escaped San Francisco, and to the amusement of my friends, I've chosen the Midwest as my hunting grounds for spiritual renewal.

After the collapse of my decade-long dyke marriage, I crave signs of continuity, evidence that some things won't change. I've become embarrassingly fixated on the Midwest. I've cuddled up in bed with *O Pioneers!* , with field guides describing the bluestem grasses of the undulating prairie, snuggled with heartland recipes and pictures of silos framed against twilight skies. I've now turned fantasy into reality, and toast my new friend.

Sally's cheeks bulge with smiling pride; she has me on her turf. So far, she's revealed little. In fact during her three month stay in San Francisco, besides our writing workshop camaraderie, we shared only a burrito and a walk through the Castro. She had managed to get a detailed description of my mercurial sex life, but hadn't said much about her own, other than briefly mentioning her very friendly, butch lover who lived on Valencia Street. Then, right before Sally left to go back to Minneapolis, she admitted to me she was going home to a husband who knew nothing of her other life.

Again Sally avoids talking about herself, so instead we discuss the people in the restaurant. A giant, curly-blond man sprawls in his chair, talks with his friends, and catches my attention. He lacks any sense of display; missing is the forced, performers' stance that I'm used to seeing in San Francisco, that give-me-a-good-time or give-me-death look.

"His story is boring," Sally says, "everybody here shares it." She drops her head to one side, lets her hair, high-school long, drag over her bare shoulder, her sleeveless white dress. Most had grandparents who left Germany or Scandinavia to farm in America and sacrifice everything for their kids. I ask if those born in Minnesota tend to stay here. When she tells me yes, I look around the restaurant, wondering if I've ever been anywhere where the people share common roots. As a native of the San Francisco Bay Area, I'm not exactly used to uniformity.

"My fierce little aunt was unusual in that she rode a train forty miles away to go to college. She even had a short period of wanting to write." Sally's pride shows at this, but it's a pride that could be measured in quarter-teaspoons. "I think part of the reason I married my husband was because I loved celebrating holidays. All the Swedish customs. I lo-o-ove that."

"Does it make people here happy—all that tradition?"

"Very." Her answer fills me with longing. I have always longed for what I don't have, even when I know I couldn't stand having it.

"Aren't you suffocated?"

"I've had my writing and haven't had kids, so I've felt just enough on the outside to survive."

And, I wonder, what about the lover in San Francsico?

After finishing our lentil soup and noodles, Sally takes me on a drive to explain why she loves it here. We arrive at a lush city park that winds along a river. Trees canopy the park's paths; their round leaves still green and juicy from spring rains. I spot a bird's nest high in a birch, the remnants of a stone wall. It's not far from what I passed driving from the airport—the rows of old mills along the Mississippi River, the many smoke stacks and arching bridges—but here the grounds are preindustrial and protected. She tells me she walks the park every day; loves it most during snowy winter afternoons, when she has it all to herself.

A nearby house reminds me of old-fashioned children's books. Three floors reach to a broad-shouldered roof; mullioned windows gleam next to the dark brown shingles; fat corner pillars brace the entry way. I imagine interior banisters, attics, pantries.

"The houses are like old trees," Sally says. "Firmly rooted."

As we leave her car and walk along the sidewalk, the weather itself increases a sense of stasis, impermeability. The air does not move; it is warm, humid, and weighted. Not many people are out, but we do see one family—daughter, mother, grandmother—looking permanently attached to their comfortable chairs on the front porch. Talking and drinking Pepsi, the mother and grandmother grin at us and continue their conversation.

～

Restless, after Sally drops me off, I decide to take my chances—with twelve-year-old kids and over-anxious police. I walk the two blocks from my hotel to Minneapolis' largest gay bar.

It's an enormous place with a maze of separate dance rooms and deejays. Almost all empty. I sit in the first room and watch a beautiful Thai go-go dancer. His pretend dick is so large under his G-string that I can't stop trying to guess its weight and density. His butt is smooth as an apple. The other men watching are also by themselves, and there are no conversations. The barboy is the most mobile person in the room. He nods and smiles an amphetamine "Yes," to my every question.

To my immediate right is a child-molester poster-boy, slobbery jowls hanging, his gaze transfixed on the dancer's dick. Near the door is a pretty punk boy; torn T-shirt, pierced nose, long delicate white fingers. A black, sweating business man drinks a quick scotch at the bar. A stoned fairy prince in tie-dye wanders in. In San Francisco each of these people would be isolated at different clubs, each catering to their own distinct form of arrogance.

Although I've been told Minneapolis has a large gay community, I can't help but feel I am in the desert and that the people have traveled a long way to get to this one precious oasis. Less pretension and more desperation.

After about ten minutes, I escape to the deserted high-rise streets. Wandering in circles, I end up at the music hall where my guidebook says Prince was discovered. It's between sets of a jazz act.

A trio takes the stage and a man blows into his sax. The first note is unadulterated pap. I look around me. Couples nudge each other in enjoyment. An older man, with the thick knuckles of a former laborer, asks if I mind if he smokes his pipe. The African-American audience nods and sways, slightly behind tempo, to every oozing riff, to every velvet note. Subdued and contented. The saxophone, my favorite instrument of defiance, swirls in a melody as pink as roses on a wedding cake.

Next, I walk along the lake near the art museum. Tall willows rise in the moonlight. A duck flashes across with her tiny brood of white ducklings. I consider finding a dyke bar and snagging company for the night, but instead find the infamous place where Mary Tyler Moore once threw her cap, and call it a night.

~ℓ~

The next day, before I begin my long drive into the prairie, Sally and I take a late-morning walk around one of the many lakes in the city. A handful of downtown skyscrapers fringe the water's western side. While older people dangle their fingers in the water's coolness, kids wade with their plastic boats. We spread her blanket on the sand and roll up our pant-legs.

While I rub suntan lotion into Sally's shoulders, we talk about San Francisco dykes. She insists they are even more conformist than Midwesterners. Everyone she knew had the same piercings, the same judgmental politics, the same messy apartments, and the same bad day jobs.

"Yeah, but I bet the sex was better."

She smiles. I'm right. "I had fantasies of staying in San Francisco." She rolls over on her stomach. "It only took a couple months though, then I knew that my home was here."

"OK. Why?" I look at Sally, the comfortable way she moves her pale body on the sand. She seems so much younger, or maybe just lighter, here in Minneapolis.

"Home is where you know you belong."

I ask her if she belongs.

"Yes." She laughs. "And no. But nobody else knows that!" She runs a handful of lakeside sand through her fingers. "Oh, god. I had this horrible dream. Don was an uncooked gingerbread man and I kept twisting him into pathetic doughy shapes and eating him raw. Isn't that cannibal?"

"Deadly." Is she going to leave him?

"I would be expelled from his family. The whole shebang." She raises her hand to her forehead in mock horror. "What would I do?"

We look at each other for a moment. I squeeze her shoulder. Her eyes stare back with a deep blue stillness. I get a glimpse of the strength I saw in the stories she wrote in San Francisco, the interior self she doesn't share easily. "Do you have to stay in Minneapolis?"

"I love it. I could never leave."

~e~

I don't know where I will spend the night. I press the accelerator, check my gas gauge, reach for a handful of nuts to bridge my hunger for the long drive into Iowa farmland. I will keep driving till I get to the pastures, the silos and red barns that I know from photographs, but cannot begin to imagine in reality. What will be the color of sunlight, the texture of the grass, the smell of the soil in the cornfields? What will the teenage girls talk about, hidden away in small towns, slurping diet cokes in diners?

I drive into the sights and sounds and smells of my trip; the future that has no shape.

As I drive, I think of Sally on a February afternoon. She's left her writing for the day, put on her gloves, her wool scarf, her long winter coat. She treads through the high banks, eyebrows freezing, cold air assaulting her lungs. She looks at the frozen river, looks at the warm, solid houses, crosses her arms around her chest and walks a little faster. She is happy. Very.

Will she ever leave her husband? Suddenly I imagine her—back at home. She is arrested in time. Kneeling. Wrists clasped behind her back, head hanging in resignation, circled by the old family furniture.

I enter Iowa and its acres and acres of green. I wonder what makes someone call a place home. Is it the freedom to act as oneself? Or is it a connection that goes deeper than an individual claim on identity? Most of the lesbians I know in San Francisco are refugees. We left a confining past to revel in the fluidity of choice. Yet the bonds we form turn as amorphous as billowing fog in the midday sun. I long to live in a place that nourishes continuity, a place that celebrates history and community. When I think of Sally's quiet life, though, I cringe. What is it I really want? Freedom or belonging? I want to cruise Valencia street late at night and hear music and poetry spilling from tiny, packed bars. I want to see the Mexican mariachis as they stroll home, lonely, with their huge, silent instruments. I want to smell the ocean on the wind. I want to see the rough-shaven skulls of women knock together on the dance floor. I want to be around people who know the fear and joy of falling off the edge. And yet, crazy fool, I yearn for family, a place, a home that feels as stable as the roots of trees.

∾

Home-phobia

Let's face it. We're home-wreckers. Like everyone else, lesbians are born into perfectly respectable homes and showered with a particularly American brand of parental love that immediately dries up when they find out we're gay. How, our parents ask themselves, did my daughter manage to slip through the cracks of the divine scheme of heterosexual propagation? They search back through their memory banks, wondering if we had stayed home sick the day they taught decency in the local public school.

We had, in fact, missed that particular lecture on decency, but certainly not because we were at home. (We actually played hooky from home whenever possible.) That was the year before Peggy Sue discovered boys, and we had been making out in the bathroom, giggling the way little girls do to hide the throbbing intensity of preadolescent titillation. Needless to say, Peggy Sue, who later became president of the PTA, remembered to borrow the lecture notes from Donald. But having learned very early on that survival as a lesbian meant ignoring the lessons of traditional morality—the family values of the American Heterosexual Home—we just blew the whole thing off and made up the points with an extra credit report on Susan B. Anthony.

No one is immune to the havoc we wreak on the home. Even mothers, whose love is renowned for its constancy, turn their backs on us. The expression, "that is a face only a mother could love," does not apply to us. Our mugs just make them feel guilty, as if something they did or did not do is responsible for our deviation from the straight and narrow. Where others "can never go home again," we were never there to begin with.

Parents think we commit ourselves to being gay just to defy them. There's hell to pay for embarrassing them in front of their bridge club friends and robbing them of their rightful 8.6 grand-children. Lesbians are such a terrible threat to the whole notion of home itself that once we have wrecked the home of our birth, we are forever punished by not being allowed to establish our own homes as adults. Picket fences and tea cozies are strictly off-limits. Forever. If we do somehow manage to set up housekeeping with another woman, our parents stay in hotels when they come to visit. They dine out rather than taking the chance of eating a lesbian home-cooked meal. They refuse to step foot inside dwellings where there is no master in the master bedroom. To do so would be to countenance the whole sordid arrangement.

Even stricter ground rules apply when we visit our parents in the family homes we grew up in. We can do what we want in the world at large—it's a free country (!)—but by God they're not going to let us sleep in the same room if we haul our partners home for the holidays.

Homeless in the most profound sense of the word, no wonder we are the queens of serial monogamy. The divorce rate among lesbians is second only to the birthrate of the moral majority. Try building a lasting relationship without having a home to hang your hat in, let alone your heart. Like sailors, we find a different girl in every port, and any port in a storm. Promiscuity isn't a luxury; it's a last resort—a desperate attempt to find a primitive home in the soft, dark caves of women's vaginas. At least they are temporarily more hospitable than the childhood homes that ejected us like foreign, incompatible organ transplants.

If making love to a woman is like trying to crawl back into the safe cozy womb of our original homes, then we should at least be credited for our persistence. Like infant marsupials burrowing into pouches, over and over we try to love our way back to the womb. Apparently we forget that we were expelled from there, too, when our nine-month lease expired.

Nothing is more threatening to the ethics of the home than our sexuality. Historical and archetypal examples abound. For one thing, "Home" is an Oedipal institution. According to the convoluted logic Freud constructed to protect the home from homosexuals, our development was arrested at the stage of loving our mothers, which we then project forever onto other women. Lesbian love is considered infantile, and of course children can't get mortgage loans.

Even male homosexuals are less subversive than we are because they do not directly violate the exalted mother that the home was erected to simultaneously protect and imprison. The home is the shrine of the Angel of the Hearth—the domestic Angel that launched a thousand ships and inspired centuries of holy wars fought for the sake of the divine mother and child who grace every hearthstone. Magnified by hyperbolic homophobia, our lesbianism is a symbolic event rather than a personal preference. Supposedly, we have the nerve to want to deflower this symbolic virgin mother with our tongues. Rape and pillage are sacred compared to our terrible lingual transgression, which flies in the face of the original emblem of Western culture, the home at the end of Odysseus's epic quest to found civilization as we know it.

When Virginia Woolf espoused the rights of women, she advocated attaining a room of our own, not a home. In fact, she insisted that for women to progress, to evolve into bona-fide human beings, we would have to kill the angel of the house, the prototype of gorgeous submission. But given the rigid dichotomies of Western culture, if you're not an angel of the hearth, technically speaking you're a murderer, a feminist, a siren, a Medusa, a witch, or, worst of all, a lesbian. Where the angelic mother rocks the cradle, we rock the boat. Though the angel seldom ventures beyond the sacred threshold of her home, we are forever hopping onto our broomsticks and other symbols of transgressive mobility. But are we liberated from the confines of the home, or doomed to wander forever and ever without even a closet for our brooms, let alone a whole house to call home?

Why do you think they burned lesbian witches at the stake? Because the grave is a final resting place, a home for the corpse to sleep until final judgment unites body and soul in glory. No such heavenly home for the lesbian's disembodied spirit, all that remains of the martyred specter of female desire.

When the Wicked Witch of the East, who was a lesbian in real life, was murdered in *The Wizard of Oz*, she was squashed by Dorothy's home plummeting from the heavens. There's no place like home to kill a lesbian dead in her tracks. I rest my case.

Given this horrific legacy, no wonder we're ambivalent about home. Historically it has scapegoated us with chronic regularity. Personally, it rejected me once and seems likely to do so again. The precedent of my family's antagonism still ringing in my ears, sharing a home with people always spelled danger—the danger of intolerance and censure and even the threat of being sent to a shrink to be cured of my monstrous sexual proclivities. Some particularly resilient lesbians may get over this primal betrayal, but I find it hard to embrace home after such a devastating rejection. I wouldn't have said that fifteen or maybe even ten years ago. In my early days as a lesbian I used to think that I had emerged unscathed by the fiasco of my upbringing. I suppose we all hope that we can escape the tyranny of the past.

With what blind optimism I finally left home, not tumbling gently from the nest but catapulting out of there with the force of the combined horror of my parents and my own angry astonishment at their rejection. I truly believed that having been crucified on the cross of sacred family values, having been branded the scapegoat not only of my own family but also Public Enemy Number One of homes everywhere, I could still just waltz into the world and set up my own home, creating a nurturing loving environment out of a void. I wanted so much to believe that I could leave everything behind me, tied up in a tight little knot of neat and tidy repression, and create the home I had never had. But mere mortals cannot create something out of nothing. And for me, home had been worse than a void; it had been the scene of my original crime against nature, against the family, against human decency itself. (As if the greatest crime of all was not withholding parental love.) The very locus of my guilt was the home. And when I finally fled my family, no one was ever as horrified again by the way I love. Without a doubt, home was the most inhospitable place I had ever been.

To this day, the most unmitigated joy I have ever felt was watching my hometown disappear through the window of the plane that finally rescued me. I couldn't wait to graduate from high school, so I enlisted as a foreign exchange student, the first in a series of stints abroad. The fact that most high school exchange students are gay attests to the fact that we are desperate to escape as quickly and as far away as possible. But the homing instinct is strong, even when there is no home to return to. I will never forget the feeling of finally wanting to go home and knowing that this place—whatever it was—did not exist for me.

The idea of home—as an abstract concept—obviously appeals to me on some profound human level, yet the actual practice or event of the home terrorizes me. For home is not merely a place; it is an act of emotional faith I just don't have. The minute I finally feel at home with someone, a terrible primal plot begins to unfold and I suddenly start fearing for my life. Made unspeakably vulnerable by proximity if not intimacy, I am stalked by the predatory memory of the trusting and defenseless lesbian child who had no idea that she could be threatened inside the nest, let alone that the main threat was the nest itself. Besieged and frightened, I lash out, fending off destruction by destroying everything in sight.

I have lost count of how many homes I have set up only to wreck. Over and over again, I beat home to the draw, shooting it square between the eyes before it even has time to reach for its holster. And then I stand, smoking pistol in hand, watching yet another perfectly beautiful, perfectly wonderful, absolutely fed-up lover ride into the sunset and out of my life. Her only fault was that she made the mistake of moving into a home with me. Relationships that have thrived for years are ruined within a few short months the minute we step foot into a home together. More than once I have vowed never to live with a lover again, yet I always return to the scene of the crime, apparently unable to resist the subliminal temptation of inevitable destruction.

I am slow learner, but I did finally identify this domestic vicious circle. I gave it a name—home-phobia—and pledged that I would face it down. I tried to convince myself that if I confronted my fears head-on, I would eventually overcome them. I would not let the menace of homophobia make me home-phobic.

Yet I am obviously not convinced that I will ever be safe at home. When I see the bloodied head of a Gay Rights activist in Manhattan, I see the motto *God Bless This Home* lurking in the eyes of the creep carrying the baseball bat. When I see a young lesbian crying because she's still in high school and can't leave home yet, I see *Home Sweet Home* embroidered and framed on the wall of her parents' bedroom. Far from needing my own home, I'm searching for a refuge from all the thousands of homes whose property taxes passed Amendment 2 in Colorado.

Thank God you can't go home again. If there's no place like home, that at least is a blessing.

But, you may say, I'm bitter if not hysterical, stuck in destructive patterns. You cite Wilma and Betty who set up housekeeping just last week and *they*, at least, feel that their pad on the Upper West Side of Manhattan is a home. They, at least, have not two but four cats and two juicers—doesn't that count for anything?

You've heard the expression a house does not make a home. Well neither do pussycats make a home, though with four you might qualify as a kennel which is, at least, a home for animals. Yet I am mindful that there are exceptions to every rule and that perhaps, if anywhere, lesbians in groups of two might be able to cohabitate in places like Manhattan and San Francisco, but only in certain neighborhoods and on certain gay days, following rules as complicated as alternate side of the street parking. But yes, it can be done, especially if we are pretty and wear dresses and makeup and heels.

My lesbian friends lament my home-phobia. They argue that since the home is a heterosexual political institution, then lesbians setting up housekeeping have accomplished the most subversive act in the history of domesticity. Yet this sounds suspiciously like joining them rather than beating them. If Audre Lorde is right that "The Master's Tools Will Never Dismantle the Master's House," then lesbian homemakers are akin to feminist pro-lifers and Jews for Jesus. Straddling contradictory ideologies, they get caught in a kind of oxymoronic limbo bordering on nonexistence.

I think especially of a lesbian couple I know who were born and raised in my dusty little hometown in the deserts of southern Idaho. With all due respect to their anonymity, let's just call them Thelma and Louise. While the rest of us fled to greener pastures (in San Francisco and New York City), these two stuck to their guns and stayed home. They bought a little A-frame cottage not three blocks from their childhood homes and settled down to a life surprisingly like that of their neighbors.

Needless to say, there is no gay flag flying in their yard, the way we drape them out our windows in Manhattan. There is no apparent difference between their house and any other on the block, except that theirs is the only one with a picket fence.

On my last visit to my parents' home—the first in seven years, since like the locust my plaguey visits are fortunately few and far between—my mother drove me by this little A-frame cottage which, if anything, was the most neat and trim on the block. Its blinding white picket fence looked as though it were painted religiously every night by the elves that erase all traces of homosexuality in small Western towns.

When my mother explained to me who lived there and how the town had a cramp in its collective neck from so vigilantly trying to avert its attention away from this house and all it represented, I detected for the first time a note of gratitude in her voice. The parents of these two lesbians pretended not to know, as if they believed economic necessity had compelled the two girls to purchase a house together. Such a colossal feat of repression would have just killed my mother who, like me, is hopelessly wide awake and almost constitutionally incapable of sweeping things under the carpet as if they simply didn't exist, just for the sake of oblivious peace of mind. And of course the whole town was wise to the truth, and surreptitiously scandalized.

I realized as my mother finished her tale that the typically circuitous point of the story was to thank me for sparing her all this—to thank me for leaving her home intact by taking my life elsewhere, far away from the picket fences of Woodlawn Avenue where prying eyes could invade the sanctity of her own hearth. The gratitude in her voice sounded to me like the love that had stuck in her throat all these years. It was the moment of reconciliation I had always been looking for with my mother. And it was all made possible by the fact that I did not try to hold on to my home—did not try to use the home as the foundation of my life as a lesbian.

When I let Mom drag me to church the next day and I saw Thelma and Louise in the next pew, I couldn't help thinking of bulls (and bull dykes) in china closets. They were obviously afraid to even look at me. After the service, I walked toward them to chat, but they ran wee-wee-wee all the way home. At least their dyke radar was still intact, but they used it to steer clear of me, as if they might be identified as lesbians by mere proximity to a big bad New York dyke. Their house was not a home; it was a closet.

I'm not saying lesbians shouldn't live in Idaho. A part of me actually admires their tenacity in staying in their hometowns. But the vision of that little A-frame haunts me with images of the constrained and finally even deformed existences of people living contradictory lives in homes that cannot possibly accommodate their true natures. I suspect that despite appearances, all houses are prefabricated— prefab homes that pinch and twinge the way Huck Finn's shoes always did, far too stiff and rigid to allow the freedom he loved so dearly.

I'll probably never transcend my home-phobia. Home life is not for me, whether it's in Idaho or in Manhattan, whether it's intrinsically conservative or radically subversive. I'm not sure we can ever be truly free of the propaganda that surrounds the home. So like Huck Finn, who was a lesbian in real life, I'm lighting out for the territories to escape the insidious intolerance of the American Home. If the cowgirl can find her home on the range, then so can I.

ROBIN BECKER

~ɘ~

Beloved Places

> *"Each of us has a vocabulary of personal transcendences. We invoke them here with one or another mantra that for us centers some ultimately desirable there. Merely pronouncing such a word feels wealthy; it closes at least part of the distance between us and some apparitional wish."*

—REG SANER

1

Flying from the east to the southwest is all gain: time, light, heat. This year I do it late, July, when the temperature at the Albuquerque airport is ninety degrees. I wait curbside for for the shuttle to Taos. A Christian Fellowship group touring mission churches gathers near me. They sit on their bags while the white-collared priest assigns each a number s/he will shout aloud, during roll-call, into the dry, still air.

∾

Jogging along the running road, I hear the sharp squawk of a bird. Another squawk. On the barbed wire fence separating me from a prairie dog town sits a burrowing owl. I stop to stare and it squawks again, oddly aggressive for a desert owl. The owl bobs up and down, the characteristic dance of these small predators. I remember a female cardinal scolding me in Carolyn's front yard for coming too close to the nest she'd built in a bush above the mailbox. In my own backyard, in the thick vines of the grape arbor, baby birds slept, their orange beaks visible at the edge of the nest. When I crossed the yard, the mother soared low and cast her shadow before me.

Stretching her wings three feet across, the owl rises and flies to a distant section of the wire fencing. I scan the prairie dog holes nearby, knowing how easy it is to confuse an upright prairie dog with a desert owl. When I find them, the baby owls are unmistakable. They stand beside their burrow like well-behaved children waiting for mama. Downy breasts. Intelligent, curious faces. Like their mother, they bob and swivel their heads around. I stand for twenty minutes, studying the birds, wishing I had a pair of binoculars to look more closely at their eyes.

∾

Beneath the shapely silhouette of Taos Mountain, my friend Alice has a riding lesson. Her dressage teacher softly calls *balance, balance, lovely* as she guides the eighteen-hand horse into an extended trot. I glance up at Taos Mountain and down at my friend here on earth. The sun beats down on her bare head and arms. The horse glistens with sweat. Their connection is exact, invisible to the naked eye, like the peace I feel living in the art colony's adobe home beneath the bald outcrop of that familiar rockface.

Though it feels close, the mountain is a one-hour drive and then a six-hour hike from the parking lot in the ski valley. Today a line of snow bisects the mountain's peak, as a blaze divides the horse's face. Last week it snowed. Down here at eight thousand feet, it's eighty-five degrees; I imagine the conditions up there: forty degrees, winds gusting from the north, trails slippery with ice. Years ago, a friend and I backpacked down from a cold overnight. We had to climb a ridge to find the pass to the trail. Hail pelted my face and chest. Wind caught my pack and pushed me backwards with each step. We made slow progress towards the ridge, slipping and sliding on the loose gravel. Two hours later, through the trees, I saw Taos shining like Jerusalem in the distance.

～

Even stranger than the way weather violates our expectations are the climatic and geographic conditions that make it possible to see weather arriving or departing. Native Americans created the phrase *walking rain to* describe the way showers *walk* across a mesa, darkening the space above the earth and then moving on.

~~

Whenever I can, for as much of the summer as I can save, I return to a funky adobe with crumbling walls at the Helene Wurlitzer Foundation in Taos, New Mexico. I love the sixty-year-old cottonwoods, hanging their enormous willowy branches into streets and patios and walkways. I find comfort in the way the girths of the cottonwoods refute barbed wire, meant to keep everything green from spilling into the winding running road to Henry's house. I love setting up a makeshift summer writing studio—a few books, wildflowers in a jar, no phone. I love knowing that on the racks in the Taos Bookshop, I'm liable to find the notecards I want, reproductions of paintings by the early Taos painters: Adams, Beringhaus, Blumenschein, Couse, Dunton, Higgins, Phillips, Sharp, Ufer. I love the sound of pickup trucks, bolts loose, bumping down and up the unpaved roads. Magpie and flicker, common southwestern birds, raise a great racket all morning in the cottonwoods. All gain.

2

I set the places I choose alongside the homes I inherit. My parents gave me suburban Philadelphia and the New Jersey shore. Memories of each inform my poems. They are the sites of an original *forbear-ance:* places in which I glimpsed the wide possibilities of the world; places where I cultivated what I later understood to be a child's first premonition of flight. On the grounds of my suburban, Quaker school, I loved the maple trees, the familiar cycles of their changing. From *Quaker Meeting, the Sixties*:

> …The fall that we were seventeen
> we scuffed our loafers on the gravelly path
> from the Meetinghouse, while maple and elm
> leaves sailed around our shoulders
> like tiny envelopes, our futures sealed inside.
> Despite the war in Vietnam, I felt safer
> than I ever would again. Perhaps
> those aged, protective trees had cast a spell
> on us, or maybe the nonviolent Quaker God
> had set up a kingdom right there—
> suburban Philadelphia…

At the same time, I felt trapped by the unexamined recitations of Philadelphia history and the overdetermined (middle-class, hetero-sexual) prospects for my life. I believed such scripts, with their pre-dictable narratives, too narrow and confining for the person I was becoming. I had no Jewish, lesbian role models when I was growing up. Only now, years later, can I begin to understand what Philadelphia—word, history, geographical place—means to me. When I can experience Philadelphia as a source of power, as well as a site of loss and sorrow, I can employ it more fruitfully in my work:

A History of Sexual Preference

We are walking our very public attraction
through eighteenth-century Philadelphia.
I am simultaneously butch girlfriend
and suburban child on a school trip,
Independence Hall, 1775, home
to the Second Continental Congress.
Although she is wearing her leather jacket,
although we have made love for the first time
in a hotel room on Rittenhouse Square,
I am preparing my teenage escape from Philadelphia,
from Elfreth's Alley, the oldest continuously occupied
residential street in the nation,
from Carpenter's Hall, from Congress Hall,
from Graff House where the young Thomas
Jefferson lived, summer of 1776. In my starched shirt
and waistcoat, in my leggings and buckled shoes,

in postmodern drag, as a young eighteenth-century statesman,
I am seventeen and tired of fighting for freedom
and the rights of men. I am already dreaming of Boston——
city of women, demonstrations, and revolution
on a grand and personal scale.

    Then the maitre d'
is pulling out our chairs for brunch, we have the
surprised look of people who have been kissing
and now find themselves dressed and dining
in a Locust Street townhouse turned cafe,
who do not know one another very well, who continue
with optimism to pursue relationship. *Eternity*
may simply be our mortal default mechanism
set on *hope* despite all evidence. In this mood,
I roll up my shirtsleeves and she touches my elbow.
I refuse the seedy view from the hotel window.
I picture instead their silver inkstands,
the hoopskirt factory on Arch Street,
the Wireworks, their eighteenth-century herb gardens,
their nineteenth-century row houses restored
with period door knockers.
Step outside.
We have been deeded the largest landscaped space

within a city anywhere in the world. In Fairmount Park,
on horseback, among the ancient ginkgoes, oaks, persimmons,
and magnolias, we are seventeen and imperishable, cutting classes
May of our senior year. And I am happy as the young
Tom Jefferson, unbuttoning my collar, imagining his power,
considering my healthy body, how I might use it in the service
of the country of my pleasure.

~e~

Atlantic City. By day we had the sand, the beach, the waves. The
beach was home. Ice-cream men hauled, on their sloping shoulders,
the white freezer cases filled with creamsicles, fudgesicles, popsicles.
My *Bubbie* set up her beach chair and umbrella. *Come here, girls,* my
mother instructed, taking the brown plastic bottle of Coppertone
from her beachbag. We stood as she lathered us with that unforget-
table smell. Released, we ran to the shoreline for our first buckets of
water. If one of us cut a foot on a broken seashell, my grandmother
told her to stand in the ocean. If one of us had the sniffles, my grandmother told her to lie in the sun, breathe the salt air, go for a swim.
Salt water for every ailment, my mother chuckled.

~e~

Jump! my grandmother cried as a wave lurched toward us. *Jump!* she
repeated as I gripped her hand tighter, tighter. When she'd had

enough, she walked me to shore. *Go to your mother,* she said. *Your Bubbie's going to swim.* I took a few steps up the beach and turned back. Arms raised above the water, my grandmother walked—a large force in a black bathing suit—into the ocean. When the water reached her chest, she smoothed her plain white bathing cap on her head and dove. In this moment, loosed from child and grandchild, delighting in her own body and the ocean's body, my grandmother left us all behind. How I admired her! Called by a pleasure and a home beyond us!

~ℓ~

Wellfleet, Massachusetts. In the summer of 1976, I shared a four-room cottage home with a painter, Gwen Fabricant. She didn't speak much, and at first I found her quiet disconcerting. Then, I discovered that her particular kind of silence—intimate, thoughtful, kind—made the small house grow spacious. By the end of the summer, with all our doors and windows open to the Cape Cod breezes and smells, I felt that we lived on an enormous, calm island, governed by our own benevolence. Poetry and painting anchored our home, giving the days form and shape.

3

A *Sustainable Community* the brochure reads. I make arrangements to see the development with a local woman who's bought twenty acres.

When Carolyn and I arrive at her house, I notice the crystals on either side of the Buddhist altar in Judith's living room. *I try to show the land to people who will bring good energy onto the property*, she says.

It's a twenty-minute drive to the cattle guard and carved wooden posts that mark the entrance to the land. Judith explains the ethical goals of the original owners, their desire to live in harmony with the desert. From the corner of my eye I spot what I think is a deer. Judith reaches for her binoculars. *No*, she says, *It's the antelope herd!* In a second, twin fawns appear beside their mother. A movement in the grass is a many-antlered male. Then, several others. They stare at our car and then go leaping away. *They're here to welcome you*, Judith says. *I only see them when I bring out people who really belong here.* Carolyn and I glance at each other.

We bump along the gravel road as Judith points out flags marking twenty-acre plot boundaries. *What are those birds?* Carolyn asks. Judith goes for her binoculars and pulls to the side of the road. *They're nighthawks. Look for the white spot on their wings.*

We continue. At another homesite, Judith says *That's my cistern.* She walks us through a blueprint that includes a solar greenhouse. Carolyn asks about two large piles of dirt.

Two kinds of soil additives, Judith says. *In order to plant trees and other plants out here, you have to work with the soil. Enrich it.* Carolyn, a gardener in the rich topsoil of central Pennsylvania, bends to feel the sandy dirt. Although I love the sagebrush and the wacky-appearing solar *Earthship* homes designed by Taos architect Mike Reynolds, I miss the simple shade of a tree. The forested series of hummocks in the distance comforts my eye. Carolyn stares at the miles of chamisa and cactus. Judith's eyes shine with her vision: solar homes built in harmony with the land; herds of antelope, deer, and elk galloping through unfenced acres; shade trees, vegetable gardens and flowers rising from the desert floor like orange groves in Israel.

~e~

Standing on the fence as I trotted up the running road was my little desert owl. She seemed to be cleaning herself in the brisk air. The sun had not yet reached the mountains; the prairie dogs had not emerged from their *sipapus* at the center of the mythic world. I kept running. On the way back, I scanned the fence: no bird. But on the ground, poking her triangular head from her burrow home, she wore in her feathers flecks of gold. She gleamed in the just-risen sun.

~e~

For the last twenty-five years, I've left *home* to write. Repeatedly, people ask me why I do not write at home. I've asked myself this question many times. Deep inside me is a voice that says, "Go on. Get to a clearing." I can't create a clearing out of the clutter of my everyday life. I can do it only where I am a stranger. Mediating this *strangeness* is frequency of return to a beloved place. Thus, the sight of the horseshoe curve before the final climb to Taos always signals a lump in my throat. Home is the place where I make my living; Taos is the place where I'm an artist. To myself. It's the place of transcendance where my heart can sing.

MERRIL MUSHROOM

~e~

Home Is Where My Children Think We're Rich

Home is where my children think we're rich, even though seven of us live in a broken-down, ramshackle, Appalachian house with three rooms and a kitchen downstairs, where we made more space in the attic by sawing a hole in the ceiling and building a staircase to get up there. We laid rough-cut boards from the local sawmill to make a floor and borrowed a drill from the neighbors to put up the walls, because the tough old oak, seasoned to steel hardness, defied all attempts to drive a nail. We cut squares in the walls at either end, framed them each with windows that we were allowed to take for free from a wrecked house up in town in exchange for carting off the trash; and voila, we now had a two-story mansion with space for four bunk beds upstairs under the rafters—two on each side—built from scrap wood salvaged from that same wrecked house up in town.

Home is where my children think we're rich, because in this new upstairs there is also space for a library, with shelves for all the books that have been collected, donated, purchased at sales; and even space for a play area with a two-dollar toy box from Goodwill filled with second-hand cars, dolls, boats, and assorted playtime treasures; although mostly the children play outside with twigs and stones, feathers, leaves, and, best of all, utensils from the kitchen. The children play in the hills and woods, play outside in all kinds of weather, are always strong and healthy, have creative minds, and never ask why don't we have a TV or video games or computer toys; although I must admit that my daughter craved a Barbie doll.

Home is where my children think we're rich, although seven of us live on bare-bones income, just enough above poverty to keep us from qualifying for any aid or assistance—$3.18 too much to get food stamps, $4.67 too much for free firewood, $6.85 over the limit for Medicaid (thank goodness we all are healthy). We have plenty of blankets in winter, and the children have enough clothes for all seasons, collected, donated, handed down, and purchased from thrift stores and yard sales, some clothing even comes around a second time after being passed on to neighbors—no name brands or fancy garb, but clothes the children could wear to play outside and not worry if they got torn or dirty or messed up. Home is where my children think we're rich, even after they grew old enough to want name-brand shoes and clothing like their friends.

I always kept one eye cocked for such fashionable regalia at yard sales and discount sales and price reductions at WalMart. I shopped every day of the year for school clothes and dress-up clothes, swimsuits, coats and shoes; purchased one item at a time, never was able to take the children shopping once or twice a year to buy their seasonal clothes all at one time new from the department store like their friends did.

When the fifth child joined the family, we converted the play area upstairs into a space for his bed with a donated mattress on the floor and sheets hung to give an illusion of privacy; and he thought that we were very rich, because he was the only one who slept in that bed, and it was always clean and warm, and there was always enough to eat at the house for meals and even in between, and where he came from wasn't like this. We grew a garden with lots of vegetables. We baked bread and cookies, kept chickens, fished in the creek, and hunted in the woods. We got milk from the local dairy farmers in exchange for doing child care. We got store-bought supplies on sale, through co-op or salvage, real cheap. Sometimes we did without butter or coffee or fruit juice: So what? Everyone had his or her own bed, and there was always plenty to eat.

Home is where the land goes straight up from the fold of the hollow, but there is a place flat enough to have a garden only a quarter mile up the hill away from the house. Doris Miller plowed it for us in exchange for a year's worth of pasture for his cows, except he never finished the fencing, and the cows got into the garden, and we made him take the cows away after that. We grew all sorts of vegetables and flowers in that garden; not right at first, because the ground was full of rocks and set hard like concrete after a rain, but later, after many years of putting manure and hay and other compost into the earth and pulling out forever millions of boulders, rocks, and stones.

Home is where we gathered eggs from the nests in the tiny chicken coop, where we pulled rat snakes from these same nests to release them a mile down the road and hope they didn't find their way back again, where we shoveled the chickenshit and straw from the floor of the coop twice a year into wheelbarrows to haul up to the garden. Home is where we watched ducklings break out of their eggs and peafowl spread their tails and the muscovy duck ride the tom turkey around the yard holding onto his wing with its beak, because it had been pecked by the tom once too often.

Home is where we used to shit into a pit in the ground up the hill behind the house, a pit covered over with a wooden milk crate upside down with a hole cut in the boards and a toilet seat set on it so we had the luxury of sitting down. We got hot in the sun, cold in the wind, and wet in the rain; until we found a good place to build a real outhouse and did so, built a real outhouse with a seat and roof and walls and even a door, with a spectacular view of the woods across the road. We used it for years until, tired of freezing our butts in winter, we converted a tiny closet in the downstairs bedroom of the house into an indoor privy.

We dug a pit in the dirt beneath the house—the house that sat up on posts so high in front that you could walk underneath it standing up straight. The children loved to play in the dirt under the house, even in the places where the hill comes up close to the floor joists, so that you have to bend, then stoop, then crawl, then scoot on your belly. The children would dig in the dirt, and so would the dogs, dig the dirt from around the posts so that we finally had to fill in those places with concrete and stones to keep the house from falling down. After we finished the pit for the privy, we cut a hole in the floor of the closet inside the house, topped it with another wooden milk crate (the one from outdoors had long ago rotted), sealed it tightly with used plastic sacks and caulking, and ran a stovepipe from the pit out through the roof of the house to carry away the odor. Next to the box we kept a can of cedar sawdust—one scoop on every poop to cut the smell even more and disinfect. Then the children thought that we were *very* rich, because we had an indoor toilet.

Home is where my children think we're rich, even though we hauled our water in jugs and buckets up the hill from the spring, and every time it rained we'd race onto the porch with every jug and pot and bucket we could find to catch the water that ran from the broken gutter under the roof, to save trips to the spring while we used the rainwater. Besides, it was fun. I could bathe and shampoo five children in three gallons of water heated on the woodstove and get them squeaky clean; bathe them in two shifts—the two bigger and then the three smaller ones together—in a dented washtub using a watering can as a shower, then carry the dirty water outside to spill on the flower beds. Myself, when I came home grimy from my job on construction, I'd carry a pot of hot water out back of the house to my pallet and table, with my soap, loofa, washcloth, and towel. I'd scrub quickly, in the privacy and quiet of outdoors, with leaves blowing in the trees overhead and the evening wind very chilly on my skin.

When we finally laid a length of black plastic pipe to feed water down to the house from the other spring that was up the hill, feed it down to the house and into the kitchen where it actually flowed into the sink when we opened the tap, the children thought that we were wealthy beyond their wildest dreams; but one day even greater riches came our way when someone gave us an old bathtub, and we converted the back storage room to accommodate it, drilled a hole in the floor to lay a drain pipe that ran into the gully and screwed a hook into the ceiling to hang the watering can from. Then we had the luxury of a real shower at last, in a room of its own, at least when the weather was warm. When the weather got cold enough, the back room would freeze, and again we bathed in the old washtub in front of the woodstove.

Home is where my children think we're rich, because after we had water running down to the house, we didn't do laundry by hand like the neighbors; we didn't even go to the laundromat anymore but bought a real washing machine on time payments. We got clothesline pulleys and ran a clothesline from the front porch into a tall tree across the road, so we could hang all our laundry out to dry, up high enough that the children could run in the yard underneath, without even having to leave the porch. We appreciated this, since we didn't have front steps anymore; when the first set of wooden steps out front rotted, we built another; and when they rotted, we built another; and then we didn't build any more, but, when the third set of steps got too rotten to use safely, we tore them down and scrapped the wood and only used the back steps after that forever.

Home is where my children think we're rich because it's warm in the winter with the old woodstove crammed full of bark ends from the local sawmill mixed with hardwood logs, where we learned that willow wood and elm do not burn well, learned that fact when one of each fell down in the front yard, and we were so happy because we thought we wouldn't have to climb into the hills for a while to cut firewood; but when we filled the stove with the willow and elm, the fire went out and everything froze. After that we climbed the hills again in order to cut oak, hickory, osage orange, and hackberry that we knew would burn hot; and the house was warm even though it was so barely insulated that the snow melted off the roof right away. We cut down drafts in the house by boring a hole in the floor in front of the stove, so that air the fire pulled as it burned came from the hole and not from every other crack and crevice in the house.

Home is where my children think we're rich, because we borrowed a sander and polished the old hardwood floor until it was beautiful, even though a log fell out of the woodstove one day when no one was home and burned a hole through the floor. The walls were beautiful too, because we pulled down our ancient barn, which was falling down anyway and nailed the barnwood up inside the house— the weathered, gray, wormy chestnut boards that people who had a lot of money would pay eighteen dollars the board foot to buy, but that we got for free. Our tables were made from old cable spools that we varnished until they shone, and we had a huge sofa made from two old mattresses piled together on a frame of scrap wood set up on cinder blocks. Upstairs we carpeted the floor with beautiful colored squares that we got for free out of the dumpster behind the carpet store, plus one huge piece of real, almost-new rug that we salvaged from where it had been thrown away because an office was refurnishing.

Home is where my children think we're rich, even though the yard is bare from their running feet wearing off the cover of fescue and plantain, until always it will be dust in the dry weather and mud in the rain. The creek runs by the front of the house in wet weather, flows down the hill and over the rocks, and when the fourth child came to live with us, his five-year-old eyes lit up and his hands rubbed together with glee at the sight, and he exclaimed "Oh, look at all the dirt! Look at all the water!"

And then the glow dimmed, as he added, "Never, never, never play in it, right?"—poor city child—but blazed again at the assurance that yes, of course he could play in it. And play the children did, in the dirt and in the water, unless the creek was in flood, which happened sometimes so that we could not even cross the raging torrent it became; and we were confined inside, at home, to read and sew and play quiet games together; to sing, dance, and make music; to put on costumes and makeup and do performances for one another; to cook and eat and clean up afterward.

Home is where the rope I hated hung from a limb of an old cedar tree thirty feet up that one of the children had climbed to tie there. The rope I hated had a knot on the bottom and dangled three feet above the rock ledge at the edge of the bank. The ledge dropped twelve feet straight down to a bed of boulders, sharp rocks, and saplings. The rope I hated was the one my children would cling to as they'd run, then leap off the ledge and swing out and around in a huge arc to end up on the bank again. They'd swing in the snow and the rain when the rock was slick, didn't check often enough if the rope was wearing thin by rubbing against the branch where it was tied. They'd swing out far and wide, never holding on tightly enough to suit me. Sometimes they'd swing two of them clinging together, and I couldn't watch for long. But all the years they used it, the rope I hated never broke, and no one ever fell.

Home is where my children went to free school together with lots and lots of neighbor kids from thirty miles around, went to school in an old log house where they were taught by all of us grown-ups in our turns, each taking responsibility for teaching what we knew best—reading, math, geography, astronomy, drum making, meditation, healing, dance, music, carpentry. The children were grouped roughly by age, babies through teens, bigger ones helping smaller ones. All together, we'd gather black walnuts and dogwood berries to sell to the local nurseries in order to raise money to buy school materials that we couldn't make ourselves, like pencils, paper, and letterhead stationery; but we didn't need much. And when Perly came to do dance lessons with the children and asked them to get in line, they didn't understand what he was talking about.

Home is where milkweed and thistledown blow through the air in the summer like snowflakes blow through the air in the winter, where trees in the spring put out foliage in pastel beginnings that preview with muted reflection their brilliance to come in the fall. Home is where we have good neighbors, where we help one another, where we work together and play together, where babies are born and no one has died yet. We have hayrides and barn dances, ball games and potluck dinners. We swim in the creek, play music, blow bubbles. We help the local sharecroppers plant and harvest. We build and demolish, do hay and fight grass fires. We go to dinner parties and dessert parties, costume parties at Halloween and Purim, and the great pie-in-the-sky party at Candi's where we all brought two pies—one to eat and one to throw at each other—what a mess—and the kids got to throw water balloons at the grown-ups.

Home is where my children think we're rich.

LIZ GALST

~~∾~~

Dating the Goyim*

On my answering machine, her voice is dark and silky, confident and reassuring: "Hey, Liz. This is Amanda Davis. I sat in on some of the panels you did at OutWrite," a lesbian and gay writers conference, "and I was wondering if you want to get a cup of coffee sometime, or lunch. Talk about what you're working on."

It's been a long time since someone's called me up for a cup of coffee, a long time, I think, that someone's gone out of her way to get my unlisted number.

What could be so bad, right? It's only a cup of joe. The worst, I'll lose an hour; these days I have a couple to spare.

---

* The words goy, goyim, and goyishe are Yiddish for gentile (singular noun), gentiles, and gentile (adjective). Some people use them pejoratively. That is not how I intend them.

We arrange to meet at a coffee bar around the corner from my house. "How will I know who you are?" I ask.

"I'm six-one and have curly, red hair."

Is she ever six-one with curly, red hair! Little ringlets, actually, freckles, almond-shaped eyes, glasses the color of the sky in autumn. Then she's got this perfect complexion, like a child's, the kind of skin grown-ups don't have.

There's something about her—not a cause for enthusiasm necessarily, but I notice it in the way she carries herself on the walk from the counter, or maybe it's her professional polish, or the glass charms she wears on a thin, gold chain around her neck—but I'm thinking: *Catholic school.*

We sit in overstuffed chairs in the back room. Small talk. She tells me we met at a party once when I lived in Cambridge and she lived in Boston. She'd attended with her girlfriend. Her then-girlfriend, she makes a point of telling me. I have no recollection of the event.

Given the nervous wreck I generally am on dates, I'm unusually calm. Like I already have—well, not an edge exactly, but this was her idea. The dating home-court advantage.

"I really just had to get out of there," she says. By which she means Boston, a place she describes as oppressively politically correct.

After we've been talking for an hour or so, I explain I've been very sick for the past few months, a bad bout of endometriosis, a gynecological problem that's left me entirely sapped of energy.

"It's getting late," I explain. I have a midterm tomorrow. We get up to leave, and on her way out the door, she says: If you need someone to bring you soup, or you're just feeling frustrated being sick and you want to talk, give me a call.

A few days later I do.

Whether it's Amanda I'm interested in, or her offer of soup, I'm not sure, but it's something. And she's cute, I think; it's been a long, sexless year since I got dumped by an old college friend I thought was maybe, you know, the one. These days I'm checking out every opportunity, though there haven't been a lot.

On the phone, we arrange dinner and then the movies. We'll meet at my door. When she buzzes, I go down, see her in the twilight, in a handsome, dark overcoat and gray silk scarf (I'm my usual schlumpy self in jeans and a V-neck sweater). "You're all *farputzed*," I want to say. Instead, I hesitate. "You're all dressed up."

"Not really. Just the scarf."

We walk down 5th Street, the warm air of early evening all around us. It's reassuring to be with someone so big. Like if something bad happens, they can take care of you.

She asks about my day. I start telling her about some research I'm doing. When television sets became common in American households. "But wait. Before we get too far into this conversation—" I'm talking with my hands like always. "Can I ask you a question? Is this a date?"

"Why are you asking?"

"Well, I just want to know whether I need to be nervous or not."

She pauses. "Why would you need to be nervous?" As if there's nothing anxiety-provoking about being on a date.

"You're not Jewish, are you?"

She looks confused.

"We tend to be a little high-strung—as a people."

For the moment, the question of the date remains unresolved. Fifteen minutes later, as we walk down Broadway, she says no, she hadn't thought of the evening in those terms.

This I don't believe for a minute. No one stares down deep into your eyes and offers her shoulder to cry on, offers hot soup on a cold winter's night, if all she wants is to be your pal, to go to the movies occasionally.

Oh, let me say this: How good it is to walk on a date! How good it is to walk in general, but on a date it's perfect. Gives you something to do with all that nervous energy. And solves the eye-contact problem, which you might have at a coffee shop or a restaurant, because you have to look somewhere, and if you're sitting across from your date at a table, and if she's too beautiful to look at, or, say, all that eye-contact feels too intimate, too demonstrative of a desire you're trying to keep a handle on, because you're trying to get to know the person first, before you sleep with them—for these reasons walking is good.

Anyway, we're on Houston, in the night air. The traffic streams past us. Our hands rest in our respective pockets.

Apropos of a mention of her father, she tells me she was raised Catholic. She says it like it's no big deal, all those years of taking the host in her mouth. Like it's something she's discarded easily in the big city, where she's moved to become a cosmopolitan.

At the Angelika, we wait in the semi-darkness for *The Young Poisoner's Handbook*. Whatever Amanda says about this not being a date, it's hard to be unaware of how close we sit to each other in the plush, velvet seats.

During a lull in the conversation, she asks, "What other remnants"—does she say 'remnants'?—"What are the other remnants of your Jewish upbringing?"

This is just ignorance, right? Or should I be offended?

"It's not 'remnants!'" I say. "It's alive and kicking inside of me!" Still deciding whether to be outraged, I explain: "Like at dinner: the spaghetti

and clam sauce. The whole time I was eating it, I was aware it was *trayf*."
She doesn't know what I'm talking about. "Not kosher, though——" and
here I begin my disclaimer, "——to me the important part is not that I keep
kosher, but that I know what's kosher and what's not. I'm from the school
that says it's the knowledge, not the practice, that makes you Jewish."

For some reason I feel called upon to defend an atavistic
attachment. I start telling her about my mother, and how, since my
grandmother died last spring, she's been going to *shul* for the morning and the evening *minyan* to say Kaddish, the memorial prayer for
the dead, which, in keeping with the Jewish practice of religious
loophole and indirection, makes no mention of the dead at all, but
rather speaks to the glory of God. (This is no doubt because after
losing someone so close, you need a little convincing.)

The mourning period for my grandmother has just ended, I
explain, but my grandfather died in November, the same day as
Yitzhak Rabin, and so now my mother continues to say Kaddish, this
time for my grandfather.

And what a wonderful practice this is, I note: to spend every
morning and every evening in the company of people who know
the depth of your mourning, especially in a society that makes so
little public space for grief.

When the time comes, I tell her, for me to lose my parents (God
forbid!), I'll say Kaddish for them also. *Yitgadal v'yitkadash shmei*

rabba. Just hearing the words is comforting, even if I'm not sure I believe in God. Not that most Jews do. We had a bad experience during the War and it's left us kind of—angry maybe, or skeptical. Besides, among those who do believe, there are about ten different and contradictory conceptions of the Eternal. Two Jews, three opinions, so the saying goes. Whether I believe in God is not the point, I say: The point is nothing good comes of vanishing.

"Maybe the greatest contribution Jews have made to civilization—" I tell Amanda, "besides Einstein and Freud and Grace Paley—is a deep and textured understanding of what it means to lose the people and the things that are closest to you."

The lights go down and the movie runs. It's the story of a British teenage boy, a science nerd/sociopath, but a sympathetic one. I like him. He poisons his stepmother, gets hauled off to jail, gets treated by a certain hook-nosed Dr. Zeigler, whom I come to see as representative of "the Jewish psychoanalyst" in cinema. Amanda, for her part, is interested in the film as parody, having read a review which described it as a send-up of British culture.

Walking back to my apartment in a dark night turned chilly, she talks to me about her job: working with authors, helping them shape their books. I like this about her. That afternoon, Amanda and her coworkers met with a reporter from *The New Yorker* who's been covering the genocide in Rwanda. "I think he's finding it hard to think about writing a book," she says. "Of all those people, he's the one who came out alive, and to write a book and make money off it seems wrong to him."

"Survivor's guilt," I nod. She glances over at me, surprised, as if it's a concept she's never seriously entertained. I continue, "He should still write it. Tell him to set up a foundation with the money."

We talk about the vacation she's going on at the end of the week: ten days in the warm sun of the Yucatan Peninsula. And then somehow, we're on to the subject of children. I want to have them, I say, at least that's how I'm feeling this week. She starts peppering me with questions: How many? Alone or with "a partner"? (I hate that word.)

"With someone else. I couldn't afford it otherwise, and also I'd go crazy."

But this is what I don't tell her: that morning, in the shower, I started doing a little math. "Let's see, I'm thirty-three years old, and I'll have to be involved with someone for two or three years before I know them well enough to have kids with them. Which, if I met them today would mean that I'd be thirty-six. So I better get a move on." Though, standing under the water, I can't say I was thinking of Amanda.

Back at the front door of my building, she looks down at me, doesn't say much. It's all a little awkward. I'm confused about what I want exactly, and so, I guess, is she. I think: "I'm not kissing her if she won't even admit this is a date." "Well," I say, "have a nice vacation."

"Yeah, I'll call you when I get back."

Later on the phone with my friend Marcos, we rehash.

Was it really a date, or not? Actually, that's not my principal preoccupation. "Should I be offended by the Jewish thing?" I ask. Marcos isn't Jewish but he knows more about Judaism than most of the Jews I hang out with.

"Well," he says, "put it this way. She grew up in Shaker Heights, where there are—what?—a million Jews. Then she's lived in New York for how long?"

"Three or four years, probably."

"Her boss is Jewish. It's New York; she's obviously had lots of opportunities to come in contact with Jews. And she asks you what other 'remnants' there are of your Jewish upbringing! That's bordering on anti-Semitic."

"Do you think? Maybe she's just ignorant."

For slim hips, I'm willing to forgive a lot.

After the midterm, my classmates and I are inundated with statistics.

It's a funny course, the Sociology of Jewish Life in America. Thirty five day school graduates and me. Maybe it's too facile to say this, but there's a lot of curly hair and yarmulkes in that room. Young women in ankle-length skirts, opaque tights. Probably they're all straight (I haven't taken a poll) and I, the only graduate student, I'm the big dyke, though I don't think they've figured that out yet.

Even though I'm almost fifteen years older than most of them, I'm intimidated. They know so much more than I do, so much I wish I did. *Halakha*, Jewish religious law, for one thing. The *cohanim,* descendants of the high priest Aaron, are not allowed to marry anyone who's been divorced. Who knew that?

And they all speak Hebrew fluently. I, myself, could never get a grip on the language, except for fifteen short minutes in the sixth grade, when I caught it like a high, pop fly in the outfield of the packed Ebbets Field stadium, only to bobble it.

Besides that, they know how to pray. And while the Baal Shem Tov, the eighteenth-century charismatic who inspired Hasidism, said if you didn't know how to *daven,* if you didn't know the words, the choreography of prayer, it's just as good to hum along, I've always felt I was missing what might (but then again might not) be an important connection to the divine.

Before the midterm, we'd charted the rise of the American Jewish population. Wave after wave of immigration: first the Sephardic, then the Germans, then, from the 1880s until 1924, the

Eastern Europeans. The whole thing reached a fabulous crescendo in the pre–World War II era. In 1937, Jews made up 3.7% of the total U.S. population—the most ever.

Now it's 2.5% and plummeting. The Jewish birthrate is low: 1.9 children per woman, 10% below the replacement level of 2.1. On top of that, the Jewish birthrate is lower than the goyishe one, something that's been true for as long as statistics have been collected.

What this means is that in the last twenty years, the total Jewish population has remained stagnant while the rest of the country has grown 20%. And none of these statistics count assimilation: Jews who no longer identify with the tribe, despite their ancestry, despite being born of a Jewish mother, which is all you have to be, according to the *halakha,* to be one.

Some might say, "Who cares?" There's always one culture or another passing from the earth. The ancient Medes no longer rule Mesopotamia and we're probably none the worse for wear. Do we miss the Goths anyway?

But I've never felt the world would be better off without us. Diaspora Jews, in particular, I think, are an interesting culture. My interesting culture.

And so it's hard for me that things are looking bad. That things are looking really not good. In my mind, I see us engulfed, like a stone sinking in the batter of a rising cake.

Short of every Jewish woman making a commitment to have four kids, there's probably little we can do to remedy the problem. In the past, it's been immigration that's replenished and rejuvenated the American Jewish population. Now that's streamed to a trickle: Hitler got most of the Europeans and the number of Iranians and Syrians is statistically insignificant. Israelis who come tend to think of themselves as Israeli, but not as Jews necessarily. The Russians—probably as many as 200,000 immigrated in the late '70s and early '80s—never had much of Jewish identity in the first place, despite being persecuted in the Soviet Union because of their heritage. The Hungarian Hasidim, who along with their progeny constitute most of the few Yiddish speakers left in the world, came in the '50s and have kept largely to themselves.

Jews with no foreign-born grandparents, according to the extremely influential *1990 National Jewish Population Survey,* are three times less likely to identify with Judaism than are Jews with three or more foreign-born grandparents.

As it turns out, all of my grandparents—the two born in Russia, the two born not that many years after their parents got off the boat—are now dead. There is no one to talk to anymore about the Yiddish newspapers on the Lower East Side, *Der Tog*, the *Forvarts*, *Die Freiheit*. The ones my grandfather sold as a boy to help support his incredibly poor family. Did my grandparents take with them, to the other side, any hopes of a Jewish future? The nerve of them for dying!

A couple days after the date, I get a message on my machine: "Liz, this is Amanda. I just wanted to tell you I had a really good time the other night. When I get back, let's go on another date—yeah, I decided it was a date."

I save the message and over the course of the next day or so, play it back to various of my friends. All of them agree, when I ask, that her voice is incredibly sexy.

Then my parents and I drive down to Washington D.C. to visit Jonathan and Rachel, my younger brother and his wife, and, of course, the baby. Really, it's the baby—Max—we want to see most. Thirteen months old, with dark hair, blue-gray eyes and chubby cheeks, he's definitely the cutest child on the face of the earth. (I say this without the slightest bit of chauvinism, bias, or family loyalty.)

As we glide over the George Washington Bridge, I tell my parents about Amanda. My father doesn't say much, concentrating on the rain. My mother, who in the twelve years since I came out to them has gone from being resistant and miserable about my lesbianism to being the parent other people should emulate, has been down this road before and is waiting to see how things turn out before she takes Amanda's goyishness seriously. Should I get the ring, she'll have plenty of time to start worrying.

Just over the bridge in Jersey City, my mother tells me that Rachel's brother's wife, Jessica, has just given birth to a baby boy. They live around the corner from Jonathan and Rachel, and I'm excited I'll get to see them, that I'll get to see the new kid.

"Who are they naming him after?" I ask as we roll down the Turnpike. This is before I remember Jessica isn't Jewish, and maybe WASPs don't name babies after departed relatives in the way the Ashkenazi do. That beautiful, sometimes circuitous way that brings the past into the present, that helps you carry it along with you. Maybe, even though Rachel's brother Billy is Jewish (as Rachel is), Billy and Jessica aren't naming the baby after anybody.

In fact, my brother Jon and Rachel, Jewish though they may be, didn't really name Max after anybody either. When Rachel was pregnant, they told my mother they were going to name the baby Max if it was a boy and Louisa if it was a girl. This caused my mother no end of consternation, because no one had been named after her grandmother Sarah, who died more than a decade ago. And, of course, my mother blamed herself for this, because while my older brother is named David Stuart for my father's father Samuel David (Stuart not Samuel, because, my mother says, "In 1960 you didn't want to use an old-fashioned name like Sam," though what she really means is in 1960 you didn't want to use a Jewish-sounding name like Sam. Now she wishes she'd done things differently) and I am named

Elizabeth Amy after my great grandfather Avram Ezra, whom everyone called Ezra, Jonathan is not really named after anyone. My mother just liked "Jonathan" and wanted my brothers to be close, like their namesakes in the Bible.

But during Rachel's pregnancy, when it seemed their child wouldn't be named for anyone, and that my great grandmother wouldn't get a name, my mother took to blaming herself for setting a bad example with Jonathan, which he was now following. And so for months, while Rachel was pregnant (this was before both my maternal grandparents died and added a couple new names to the list of the unspoken-for), my mother enlisted my aid in lobbying for the baby to be named for my great grandmother. I would call Jonathan on the phone and say, "Look. It's an S. Sarah. There's a lot to work with." He would mumble something, and I would say, "Jonathan, think about it. When Poppy dies"—that's my grandfather, who did indeed die last November—"when Poppy dies, there's going to be an H." (For Harry; Heschel actually. He was Heschel Feivel Rubinstein when he came to this country at age four.) "Okay, it's an S. You could do a lot worse."★

★ Not to worry. Jonathan and Rachel gave Max the Hebrew name Seriah. My parents' rabbi picked it out, and since, in the Bible, Seriah was the father of Ezra, and Ezra, you may recall, was the name of my great-grandfather, my great-grandmother's husband, my mother is now satisfied that my great-grandmother has gotten a name.

Anyway; my mother says, in answer to the question about the name of Jessica and Billy's new baby, "Daniel Isaac after Billy and Rachel's two grandfathers."

"Is he going to be a man in Israel?" I ask.

Which is my way of wondering whether he's going under the knife, whether they're having a *bris*. Maybe they're not going to raise him Jewish, and according to most Jewish denominations (though not the Reform), you're only Jewish if your mother's Jewish, which Jessica is not.

"Yeah, they're using the same *moyel* that Jon and Rachel got for Max."

It occurs to me then—moyel, bris, a man in Israel—that if Amanda were in the car with us, she'd have no idea what we were talking about.

We're in my brother's square, brick house in Silver Spring.

Things feel kind of strained here. Rachel seems tense. Plus, you can never really tell what's going on with Jonathan. "Teflon," my mother says, "nothing ever seems to bother him." He's my brother, I love him, but we don't exactly click. I think our worlds are too far apart. What I talk about with my friends—gay politics and gossip—I can't really talk about with him and Rachel. There's no common ground, except the family and especially, the baby. We talk about Max morning, noon, and night. And as much as I adore him, I start feeling a little resentful, find myself pulling back.

On Sunday before breakfast, we're hanging out in the living room, in our pajamas, reading *The New York Times*.

"How was the movie last night?" I ask my sister-in-law. They went to see *The Birdcage*.

"It was okay. I didn't realize it was going to be *La Cage aux Folles*."

Except, I say, that *La Cage aux Folles* had one major difference. Well, two. First of all, there was the big "I Am What I Am" number that isn't in the remake. And second, in the original, it's quite clear that the son is asking his fathers to betray themselves, to betray their relationship.

She stares up at me, blank-faced.

A few minutes later we're all at the breakfast table. Max, an impish grin on his face, shovels pieces of a corn muffin into his mouth. Half the muffin falls on the floor, but who cares? We get a big kick out of it.

I decide it's time to start talking about something I'm interested in and mention a forum I'd attended a couple of nights before: "Liberalism: Is it still good for the Jews?" It was a relatively civilized event until the featured conservative speakers started talking about how terrible gay marriage was. Then, in a quintessentially Jewish response, about fourteen people, from the floor, began making speeches about exactly how wrong the speakers were.

Jonathan looks a little frustrated, like: Enough with this gay stuff, I already had to see *La Cage aux Folles*.

Looking for a quick way out of the conversation, he says, though he's not particularly religious, "Are there any examples of gay marriage in the Bible?" He gets up from the table.

We start to clear the dishes.

"Well," I tell him, "David loved Jonathan 'surpassing the love of women.'" I can see this makes him a little uncomfortable, how it links him to my older brother in a way he'd rather not think about.

"And Ruth and Naomi spent their lives together, pledged their lives to each other, I think, even though they were mother-in-law and daughter-in-law."

"That doesn't necessarily mean anything," my mother says on her way into the kitchen.

"I know, but gay marriage is a new concept. The idea of homosexuality itself is less than one hundred and fifty years old. People didn't think about sexuality the same way before that. So they wouldn't have written about it in the Bible like we write about it now. I'm just saying it's open to speculation."

"Well, you know," my mother is trying to defuse the situation, "a lot of people in the Bible married people they weren't supposed to. Moses, for instance, married a black woman."

Oy! Now I'm looking for a way out: "Wasn't everybody pretty dark then?— Zipporah?" I ask. "She was Ethiopian?"

"Yes."

"And aren't the Ethiopian Jews—don't they trace themselves back to an encounter between David—no, Solomon—and the Queen of Sheba?"

Sensing it's time for a rescue, my father, who more than anyone I know understands the subtle theatrics of conversation, breaks in in mock outrage: "I think the worst"— he hesitates, aggressively waving his index finger in the air as he loads the dishwasher—"the absolute worst was that Esther. Marrying a goy!"

Of course, this is the funniest joke in the world—at least to me— because it's only by marrying a goy (in this case King Achashveros, the Persian Emperor) that Esther is able to save the entire Jewish people from annihilation.

Back in New York, I realize there's more to my father's joke. He's giving me permission to intermarry. "Lighten up!" he's saying. "More than once has our demise been foretold. But we survived. Look! I have a grandson."

I tell this to Marcos on the phone. "The thing is, the joke was one of the most beautiful, hysterical things my father has ever said. And to hear him say it was pure heaven. But it's not the kind of thing he would say in mixed company."

"Yeah"—

"And if I were involved with some goy, and she were down there with us, he wouldn't have said it."

And so, in this way, going out with the goyim seems like a trade-off. One kind of pleasure—the absolute full-body delight of hearing my father reel off these incredible, Jewish-specific jokes—for another, the connection and pleasure you get with a girlfriend. Such are the mathematics of love.

Actually, I've dated the goyim before (I say this with no small amount of guilt in my heart, as if I've romanced the whole of Christendom), and maybe if things had worked out differently, I'd be married to one of them now—of course, not legally but de facto. These days, though, maybe because of Amanda, I've begun to wonder: if I have to subtract in order to add, will I end up losing more than I gain?

My friend Julie Felner and I sit in Casalinga, a cheap Italian place on First Avenue, eating ravioli and talking about girls.

I complain about Amanda, who, despite her vast goyishness and terrible politics, has, since she's been on vacation, occupied too much of my mental energy.

Amanda aside, I say to Julie, there are big problems with dating the goyim. The first one is Christmas trees. I don't want to live with one. I know that if I were happily cohabiting with some gentile, it would be unreasonable to ask her not to have one, especially since I'd have every intention of celebrating my holidays in our house. Still, I don't care. I'm not having one.

But that pales in comparison to the issue of raising children. I want mine to be Jewish. Not just Jewish, but raised among Jews, so they'll know the inflections, the Jewish ways of making a joke.

Julie goes out with this woman named Amy, whom I really like. Amy's a goy. A real one. Her parents live in South Carolina and go to church. "So do you find it a problem?"

"No, with Amy, it's great, because I can feel I'm really Jewish. Like I'm not a fake." Julie worries she's not Jewish enough. This despite her two Jewish parents, her schnoz, her way of phrasing a statement as if it's a question. She doesn't feel like the genuine article. No doubt that's because being Jewish isn't one easily definable thing. You don't have to ascribe to any particular set of beliefs (though thinking Jesus is the son of God definitely puts you over the line). Jewishness is that complex knot of ethnicity, religion, language, observance, texts and circumstances that have formed us over the ages. As religions go, it favors learning and practice over faith. In fact, (and this I just recently learned) it's just as good to study the teachings of the eighteenth-century Goan of Vilna than believe, in the deepest corner of your heart, in the Holy One, blessed be He. Still, Julie doesn't think she knows enough. "Five Yiddish words," she says across the formica table. "I try to use them whenever I can."

This is a big problem amongst the contemporary Ashkenazi. It's only for the past couple hundred years we've been allowed to participate in Western culture. To mix with the goyim. Since then, the less observant among us have been preoccupied with the question of who we are, and some of us, with whether we're Jewish enough. This is especially true for Jews of my generation, who've mixed into a world our parents could never imagine.

Julie, particularly, doesn't have many friends of the Mosaic persuasion, and it's for that reason that she's come to refer to me—only half jokingly—as her "Jewish friend."

She tells me this as I'm finishing off the pesto. I also don't have as many Jewish friends as I'd like. "And think about it, Julie, we've both worked in publishing!" So much for that Jews-control-the-media conspiracy theory.

Anyway, Julie hopes that some of what she thinks is my encyclopedic knowledge will rub off on her. The other day on the phone, I told Marcos, "I think I'm becoming Julie Felner's rabbi."

If that's the case, American Jewry is in real trouble.

Which is sort of what my professor keeps saying in class. Study after study reveals the level of knowledge most self-identified Jews have about Judaism and Jewish culture has declined. Indices of ritual practice are low. A famous sociologist, now dead, even went out of his way to develop a theory that predicts the kind of ritual observances and practices that will survive in the U.S. Twenty years later, he's right on target.

The biggest culprit, though, seems to be intermarriage. Or maybe it's not the culprit but rather, a marker. Jews who feel peripheral to the Jewish community tend to intermarry. Jews who feel part of it don't.

Back from vacation, Amanda comes over to my house. For ten days I've been waiting for this moment, pondering what I'd do when I finally got her on the couch, which happens to be where she's sitting right now. I'm standing over by the TV.

"What did you do this afternoon?" she asks. In point of fact, I've just schlepped fifteen paperback *haggadahs* home from a Jewish bookstore in midtown for my mother, who's decided it's time we got new ones; the old ones are twenty years old.

I point to the bag. "You don't know what these are, do you?"

She looks up from the couch blankly.

I hand her the haggadah, along with a kid's version I got for my six year old cousin Melissa.

"Oh, they're the prayer book you use for Passover."

"Well, not a prayer book exactly."

What do I think I'm doing?

With all the bounciness of an excited second-grader, she tells me she's celebrating this year with some Jewish friends of her parents. She's going to learn.

She points to one of the pages in the kid's book.

"Can you read all this?" She means the Hebrew.

"Well, I can sound it out. I know some Yiddish and they're written in the same characters."

We have a conversation about the mother tongue. She thinks it's a wonderful language. So onomatopoetic and expressive. She wants to take a class.

Maybe I'm not giving her a fair shake here, but this is what I think to myself: "Who's she going to speak it with, the *Satmar*?"

A couple of nights later, a woman from a Reconstructionist shul on 86th street calls me up. The night Amanda'd left me the "date" message, I went to that forum there, the one with the Jewish conservatives—Midge Decter from *Commentary* magazine, and Jay Lefkowitz, an attorney formerly attached to the Bush administration.

At the shul I'd filled out a survey: How did I find out about the forum? Was I a member of a synagogue? The woman calls from the membership committee to see if I'd like more information and "maybe, you would be interested in joining?"

I say, well, more information, yes, why not? But I don't think I'll join. First off, I live in the East Village, and 86th Street's a real schlep. Besides, if I sign up anywhere, it'll probably be the gay shul on Bethune.

"Oh, now I remember you," she says. We fall into an easy conversation. "Ach, that Midge Decter, she's a real piece of work."

Lefkowitz was scarier, I say. "Like Decter with the gloves off."

So *haimish*, I think, so like home. The tones of voice, the staccato syntax are those I've grown up with, those I adore.

She gives me her name and number, even tells me there are a few lesbians and gay men active in the congregation. "In case you're ever in the neighborhood on a Friday night, and you want to come to the shul, you should have someone to sit with." I tell her I'll call if I'm up there.

I hang up the phone and think how at ease I feel with Jews, how at home. More at home than with anybody else. That conversation couldn't have happened with a goy, and not because of the subject matter.

Then I realize that sometimes it all feels way too much like home. And how among Jews, with my Jewish girlfriends, I've sometimes slipped without warning into the complete claustrophobia of my childhood, that terrible feeling of being trapped I experienced almost the entire time I was growing up. I wanted nothing better then than to be out of there, to disassociate myself from everything and everyone I knew. My mother told me that was impossible. "When the Nazis come again," she'd respond whenever I'd say something about not having to be Jewish, "they'll know you're a Jew anyway."

Maybe it's because of the conversation with that woman from the 86th Street shul that I start thinking a lot about my grandparents, and how I tend to consider the world they came from the real Jewish world. One that can't be resurrected.

That world thrived in isolation (though not complete isolation: Jews have always mixed, to some degree or other, with the non-Jewish peoples around them). They came from *shtetlach* in Russia. Sold kosher chickens in stalls in East New York. My uncle Morris, who's now 71, had a quadruple bypass last April and still smokes cigars (I could kill him!), arrived at kindergarten in upstate New York thinking English was a foreign language.

It's into the last gasp of that world that I was born. A *mezuzah* on the doorframe. Kosher Rokeach soap on the splashboard of the kitchen sink. My family didn't keep the dietary laws, but for many years there were no cheeseburgers on our backyard barbecue grill. We knew what you were supposed to eat and what you weren't.

More than that, I grew up surrounded by Jews. Not just my parents and my brothers, my grandparents (whom I saw almost every weekend), my aunts and uncles, but my neighbors, all my parents' friends—a lot of Jewish doctors, Jewish teachers.

These people couldn't be the goyim if they wanted to. Not that they were so religious, the people I grew up with. Once someone got a secular education, my grandfather told me, (he himself was a *cheder* boy turned accountant, thanks to City College), "You didn't want the burden of religion. You didn't want to change from Judaism, but you didn't want to go to synagogue every day."

These people wouldn't have known how not to be Jewish, nor would they have wanted to. They wouldn't have known any other way to be. Their Jewishness lives not just in the synagogue but also in their inflections, the shrug of their shoulders, they way they offer you fourteen things to eat when you walk in the front door.

My mother, for instance, says she was twenty-five before she knew there were different kinds of goyim, that Protestant was different than Catholic. These days that's unthinkable. People of my generation have more in common with gentiles: the Brady Bunch, McDonald's french fries, the English language. I know the difference between the Baptists and the Congregationalists, between MTV and VH1. We people of my generation slip so easily into the goyishe world. We know it intimately. We don't think of it as their world. We think of it as ours.

Not that much later, I make plans to have dinner again with Amanda, who's still cooing over her Mexican vacation. "I'm tanned and beautiful," she says on the phone.

Whatever happened to humility?

She climbs the stairs to my apartment; I notice she's got a new haircut. A bad one. Call me fickle, but the spell is broken. Probably I was never really that interested, just juiced up with the thought she might like me, with the impossibility of a Jewish girl with progressive politics finding love with a goy who writes polemics for a neoconservative magazine.

Not long thereafter, I decide it's time to back out of this gracefully. I tell her on the phone: "I—I—I—I just don't think this dating thing is going to work out." Still, it's a lost opportunity. I feel sad afterwards.

A couple of days later, after class, I go up to talk to my professor.

She's a knowledgeable person, well-connected to that network of sociologists who've been documenting the Jewish community's rise and fall. This week we've been talking again about intermarriage. Heterosexual intermarriage, though that's not how the sociologists phrase it.

For several sessions now, we've been studying graphs and charts, documentation drawn out in white chalk on a blackboard in the front of the room. In keeping with the not-too-optimistic tone of the second half of the semester, Professor Friedman tells us that 52% of Jews now marrying are marrying outside the community; that's up from 9% thirty years ago. In many of those marriages, the Jewish partner does retain his or her sense of Jewish identity. In the mid-`80s, some sociologists said intermarriage didn't necessarily have to signal a loss. If half the children born to interfaith couples developed a sense of Jewish identity, numerically speaking, things would work out just the same. But only one-quarter of these children do. In many cases, they feel torn between their parents' different religious or ethnic affiliations and opt instead for neither.

Professor Friedman, an Orthodox woman in her sixties, knows I'm a lesbian and seems fine with it.

"The next time they conduct the National Jewish Population Survey," I ask, "are they going to include questions about sexual orientation?"

"Yeah, I think so."

"Because gay people intermarry, too," I say.

In class, we'd discussed how different Jewish communal organizations are trying to stem the tide. Towards that end, the New York office of Hadassah, the nation's largest Jewish women's organization, keeps sending me these invites to (straight) Jewish singles' brunches at fancy venues like the Jewish Museum, or Broadway openings. And every now and again I receive from them in the mail xeroxed announcements congratulating couples like "Lisa and Joel," who met on a Hadassah Vanguard Singles Harbor Cruise, and have just recently announced their engagement. This despite the fact that I've personally told a Hadassah staffer in charge I'm a lesbian and suggested it's time they started organizing mixers with the lesbian and gay synagogue and the gay and lesbian committee of the Upper West Side Jewish Community Center and the lesbian and gay caucus of B'nai Jeshrun, a Conservative shul.

"I mean," I say to Professor Friedman, "I think the Jewish community should be just as concerned about finding me a nice Jewish girl"—Please, God, a doctor!—"as they are with finding one for my older brother."

"And they should be just as concerned about the fate of any children I might have as they are with my little nephew Max."

Professor Friedman nods her gray head. "You know," she says, "I never thought of that."

~~

After the Fall

Two weeks ago I sat at my kitchen table talking with one of my best friends, who also happens to be an ex-lover. As lesbians, this woman and I are to each other as much or more than family. Our community is made up of such relationships, we can't afford to run off and hide after each failed affair. Nor do we want to, the pain of that loss is far too great. There are new partners for both of us now, two years after our breakup, but we are still a very big part of each other's lives.

We were drinking coffee and talking, a spring rain had refreshed the struggling flowers in my window boxes. Another winter— Northern Californian style—had passed. We talked about our mothers. I had just started to realize that the delicate balance between my mother and I would soon topple, change into something I had only just begun to imagine. She is aging.

I'm just over thirty and my mother is nearing seventy. In her health it is hard to see those years. She's a Southern Californian widow: jogs three mornings a week, walks on the beach, eats health foods, square-dances with the zeal of a highschool cheerleader. She is nothing like her mother was at seventy: matronly in black dresses, infirm.

This conversation took place in my kitchen around three-thirty in the afternoon. I was talking about writing about this time in my relationship with my mother; we travel together, we camp together, we go fishing together (although this last summer I noticed she would no longer take the steep paths down near the creek for fear of slipping). We are learning from each other and still learning about each other. After some years she has come to accept my lesbianism— my "lifestyle" as she calls it—and respects my decisions, participates in my life, has relationships with my lovers and friends. In some ways I am trying to be like her and in other ways I fear our similarities. As in any mother-daughter relationship, there are complications.

After the rain stopped, my friend got back into her utility truck and drove back to her job fixing errant stoves. I made some notes in my journal—*immortality, feminism, community*. And I went off to the newspaper where I work the swingshift. That night I came home to hear my brother's deep voice wavering on my answering machine: "She'll be all right," he first assured and my limbs went cold. "This afternoon, around four, Mom fell and broke her hip." He left numbers to call.

I froze, unsure, as if my conversation had somehow caused the fall, yet knowing that was impossible. For the first time I thought of my mother's death, would she make it through a major operation? Would she lose her mobility? Her independence? Then I dialed frantically: my brother, her friends, the hospital.

Life would go on, I was told, only more slowly for awhile. Mom needed care.

My brother was due to get married in less than a week, his honeymoon would follow. After the hip operation, mother would need someone full-time in the house. To pick up and go home seemed the only choice. I couldn't imagine a nurse, a stranger in our home, although I also couldn't imagine me moving back to the small and conservative Californian beach town of San Clemente. My life was flexible, I had some time off coming to me, I was caught up on my bills, but even so it was difficult to arrange the finances and logistics. What do other people do? People who don't have back-up and flexible jobs? Women who have families to support? Children who have moved far away from their parents? Our country has no plans for looking after the elderly, and no resources. Most people are thrown into home-care situations, where strangers visit to help with bathing or meals, then scoot off, leaving the sick lonely and scared. Others are shunted into nursing homes where quality care is astronomically expensive, and even basic care drains bank accounts with frightening speed.

My mother is lucky. My life has afforded me the time and luxury of setting my Bay Area schedule afloat: I told work, teachers, editors, friends, and my lover that I was going and I didn't know for how long. It was romantic almost, that shirking of responsibilities, and no one dared press me for a return date. I wondered if it's a kind of guilt that kept them from asking: I was the dutiful daughter, a shining example of child-parent devotion.

~

And so it is as if I've been picked up from that kitchen table conversation and dropped into my hypothetical pondering. I am taking care of my mother. I am in my mother's house, the house I grew up in. My "home."

I have lived in several states, on several continents, and with several lovers, and sometimes I have called these places "home." Even so, this is the place I truly call home. It is a place I know better than any other—I could name and pinpoint nearly every plant, pet, and person who has lived in this neighborhood for the last three decades. But more importantly, it is a place where I am known. There are people here who have seen me, and supported me, through all my incarnations: Beatles wannabe, tiny swim champ, giggly Girl Scout, corner lemonade-stand salesgirl, high school cheerleader, defiant young heterosexual, world traveler, radical dyke, mellowed lesbian dog lover.

My mother's plight brings the neighborhood together. People come by, the same ones who carted me to swimming lessons, watched me build sandcastles. Their kids and grandchildren come round. We chat and catch up and then all make their way down the hall into my mother's bedroom where she reads, works crossword puzzles, rests, hold court. It is late afternoon and I've just checked in on her. She is sleeping, her browned skin slack, weathered and rich against the white and lace of the sheets.

By all accounts she is doing marvelously, nine days ago she couldn't walk and now she is creeping around on her walker, taking short rides in her wheelchair. But it is frightening to see her help-lessness. My pillar of support.

My mother.

And in a relationship that has never been close physically, it is scary to be so intimate with her body. I need to help her to bed, to the bathroom; I empty her bedpan in the mornings. For her, too, this must be difficult. A strong-minded, self-sufficient woman with little patience for disease or illness, she has found herself at the receiving end in a situation she has always abhorred. There is a strange embar-rassment on both sides. For the first few days she had jagged crying binges—partially due to the morphine. Anger and helplessness seeped out from behind her closed eyelids. I tried to comfort her but her first reaction would be to dry her eyes, point chin proudly heavenward, and announce, "I've just got to accept this. Whatever happens, happens."

I think there are fears, unspoken, on both sides. I am wondering about her old age, how we will deal with it, what will be my part in it. She too must have these questions. If she becomes infirm, where will she live? With whom? I can't imagine living at home with her, but a nursing home? Who can call those places "home?" The thought sickens me, let alone the cost. Social security hardly covers living expenses and even though she is over sixty-five, my mother's government health benefits, we are told, don't cover everything she now needs. If I hadn't been able to come home, I am also told, my mother would have managed with home help and the support of her friends. This time, she has savings, I have savings, and her injury is neither drastic nor unfixable. In time, a hip will heal....

But all this brings up so many sneaking fears, they play in my stomach and throat. I am scared of being orphaned on this planet, losing the tie that has always held me to "home" regardless of circumstances. And I am also thinking for the first time about my own old age, who will be with me? Who will rinse out my bedpan? A lover? An ex-lover? Children? Mine or whose? Will I even make it that far? Will the world?

There is so much death around us in the gay community, it's almost as if I've forgotten about old age. No one seems to get there anymore. Cancer and AIDS take those in their prime. In my mother's neighborhood these realities seem very far away. Her friends have aged, as they say, gracefully. The neighborhood "grandmother" is in her eighties. She walks daily to the corner mailbox, drives, and still bakes the best cakes in town. My mother's best friends, two women slightly younger than she, race around with grandchildren and embark on world travels. They see each other every day, for a walk, coffee, dinner, and talk on the phone. One lives two doors down, the other less than a block away. And all three women have known each other for twenty-five years.

In my first blush of feminism I pitied these women—and my mother—the way they were all sucked into marriages and families in some way without thought of their own fulfillment. But now I'm uncertain. When dissected, their community and their friendships look not unlike mine—sans the complexities of ex-lovers. I've grown to admire, almost envy these women and the simplicity of their choices. It's no wonder my thoughts of home are so free-floating; so many things in my life are constantly changing. Often I am bound by my own disappointments and confusions: no babies, no picket fence, no husband. Choices seem overwhelming—to move here or there, have a baby, move in with my lover, start a career or live marginally yet creatively?

My mother came into her current career through volunteer work and is now happy at her job, leading whale watching trips and creating marine ecology programs for children and the disabled. One of her best friends recently retired and after many years of separation her husband moved back into her home—as her roommate and best friend. The other friend volunteers as a teacher of English for recent immigrants. All three women have experienced the influence of feminism on their lives—and come out satisfied with their lots. And as far as I can see, happy. And I think about my peers, our introspective concern with divining our own destinies.

I'm thinking all this as I do the things my mother did for me: cooking three meals a day, washing her clothes, cleaning the house, grocery shopping, errands. After less than a week the novelty of her injury has worn off and at times I am almost resentful. I am also incredulous that these women—my mother—did this same work for twenty years without much acknowledgment or appreciation, let alone compensation. I remember her sitting down Sunday nights while the TV blared another episode of some Disney movie, her pencil scratching the weekly menus onto a small pad which she kept in the kitchen. Dinners, breakfasts, packed lunches, afternoon snacks. When I think of her sacrifice—which she claims felt like no sacrifice at all—I think about my own lack of patience, my selfishness.

I don't know as of yet how this will leave us, or change us, as mother and daughter. I know my mother is a fighter, but this is round one of a fight she will inevitably lose. Eventually my mother and I will talk about her death, or perhaps we won't. I am afraid. And then I know we are fortunate: there seems to be money and time enough for us to work together graciously towards whatever the future holds. But nothing is certain. There are few models for this stage of parent/child relationships. I truly wish there were. At some point I will be set adrift, whatever that might mean. I will face more choices in my life than my mother ever did and I hope I can turn out as happy, as productive, as unregretful.

I wonder what my life will look like at her age: a collection of friends, ex-lovers, memories. Happiness? Health? In the year 2031, what will define the scope of my life, my family, my freedom?

Most of all, I wonder: After she is gone, where will I call home?

~e~

An Ode to Billy Inmon

The summer that Billy Inmon went on a twenty-seven-day hunger strike on the state house lawn went by in a woolly and absent-minded heat. I rode past the state house every day on the bus from work, but could never see, and often never remembered to look for him. But I could see him on TV, pale and sickly, declaring his righteous campaign for governor from a pink lawn chair and mosquito net. Rumor had it he was fed protein drinks twice a day, as much of a hunger strike any aging politician was ever expected to endure.

I think what Billy Inmon must have known during his last stand on the state house lawn was that he couldn't survive as a politician, not in this city, however small or Midwestern it was. His most notable effort was as the director of the Ohio State Fair, but he was scorned from that job by the governor himself. He was a bigot, and even as we stared in awe while he starved himself in the 90 degree heat, we all knew it.

This was the same summer I came home from my first year of college in a daze, not from the books and papers or the calculus problem sets or even the huge industrial city that surrounded me that year, but because of a two-week affair with a woman, my first, and it had caused the fault-line of my heart to crack and spill. It was all apparent now, every little crush, every high school boyfriend, it all amounted to her, and her curly hair, her patchouli oil, her every tingling move. For the first time, my body made sense to me, sex made sense to me, and all the confusing grinding and poking that had gone on in the back seats of so many cars seemed inconsequential and far away.

But there was still the problem of summer vacation and my fanatically religious mother praying out loud on buses and crowded sidewalks; the problem of Billy Inmon and the man on the street corner with a sign that said "Judgment Day: August 13, 1994. Will you be prepared?"

This was the same summer that Hulk Hogan admitted to taking steroids, the summer that Prince Charles admitted to cheating on Lady Di. This was the summer that O.J. Simpson was chased by the police in his Ford Bronco while people pulled their lawn chairs up to the side of the freeway and held up signs that said "Go, O.J., Go!" This was the summer I vowed would be my last in Columbus, Ohio.

But first and foremost for my hometown, this was the summer of Billy Inmon, and no matter how little any of us knew of the man, no matter how little any of us knew of each other, no matter how small our common ground, we could say his name and nod. We could also say his name and laugh, say his name and agree: he must be crazy, he must believe in what he's doing, he must be eating more than they're saying, he must be hungry.

This was the summer when Billy Inmon gnawed on our stomachs and minds, my last summer in Columbus, Ohio. His hunger strike, which came about because Governor Voinovich refused to debate him, began on my birthday, August 1, 1994, and my mother's house was five blocks from the Ohio State Fairgrounds. Most of the year, the fairgrounds are a ghost town in the ghetto until those first two weeks in August when people who live along East 11th Avenue begin to prostitute their front yards shamelessly for fairgoers to park their cars. This was the muddle I walked through every day to get out of my neighborhood that August. Past the car wash and abandoned school, past the freeway ramp, past the nameless bar where they stare as I go by, and then the quarter-mile stretch of freak show they call the Ohio State Fair. This is a neighborhood that at all other times of the year is known as South Linden, which means to anyone who watches the nightly news that it is only meant to be driven through, windows rolled up, foot on the accelerator. But this is the place I had come from. This was my home.

"'You can never go home again,'" Susan, my boss, would quote to me that summer. We were choosing photos for the upcoming newsletter, and I was scanning our choices into the computer: enhancing, reducing, and polishing.

"But I *am* home, Susan. It hasn't changed a bit."

"But *you* have, and that's the problem. It won't ever be the same again."

~

"I'd like to be at home in my own bed," Inmon said in an interview one morning from a pay phone near the state house lawn. It seemed to me that if a man was going to starve himself on the state house lawn, he should have better access to the press than a pay phone. But then again, these weren't the comforts of home. He slept in a lawn chair, he showered at the YMCA. You had to respect a man for that, didn't you? But you also had to wonder what he thought about during those showers, if he thought of Voinovich in the luxury of his home, that big white mansion, the one that had turned Billy Inmon into an exile, the one that left him at the YMCA every sticky morning.

~

"Hello there," Phil said from over the chain-link fence. "Don't you try to look all innocent with me—I know your secrets. I saw you in the back seat of that car last night. Who was that guy, eh?" Phil is my mother's overweight neighbor and landlord who lives in the nicer half of our yellow-gray double on 12th Avenue. He walks with a limp—a war injury, he claims—and his rusty van, the same dirty color as the house, advertises NRA slogans across its bumper. He makes up anything he can think of about me, maybe he believes it. This is his right—he rents to my mother for what she can afford, which is almost nothing. I put up with him.

"I wasn't in a car last night," I told him. "I was on a motorcycle. With a woman." If he was going to make up stories, the least I could do was come up with my own version.

"Hmmph. Sure looked like you to me. Don't worry—I won't tell your mother on you." He offers a rusty-toothed grin.

"I told you. I was on a motorcycle with a woman last night. It couldn't have been me."

"Two women on a motorcycle—give me a break. I know it was you. Your secret's safe with me."

~·~

Addy's motorcycle crashed down 60th Street at four in the morning on Tuesday night of finals week. She had a final in five hours and I was left on the windowsill of my dorm room, the lights out, watching her trail of red taillights and smoke turn onto Woodlawn and disappear. I felt at home in my bones for the first time, but rattled, absolutely cracked open. The quarter was almost over and my flight to Columbus was less than a week away. Addy would be in Chicago, then Massachusetts, then New York, and then anywhere else she could afford.

"If you could be anywhere right now, if you could go anywhere in the world, where would it be?" Propped on her elbow beside me in the dim light, Addy was all outline and shadow. How could I tell her I didn't know? How could I tell her that I wanted to go home, that I didn't know where that was?

"I'd be here," I said and smiled. "I'd be right here with you."

"You're such a liar," she said. "Such a fucking liar." Then she rolled on top of me and kissed me until either of us could believe anything.

~~e~~

"Did you hear they're trying to tempt Inmon with omelets this morning on WNCI?" Susan asked, walking in the door that morning. This was before she noticed the ashen gray of my face, the open newspaper on my lap. They were in the hospital, two women in love, kept in separate rooms, hooked up to separate machines, but still breathing, still breathing for each other. They would be packing their bags; they were never going back to that home again. Not after being greeted by fists, not after the words, "you fucking dyke cunts" were screamed at them when they were down. They were two women from my neighborhood, the only two women in the world

I felt close to at that moment, these two women with eyes swollen against the light, these two women I had never met in my life.

∼℘∼

No matter how bad home is, the thing to remember is that you'll never find anything like it, and you'll never be happy until you find it. Nothing is as suited to you as the house you grew up in, nothing will ever feel like the street you played double-dutch or kickball on, no town is like your home town, no state like your home state. Once, on a road trip, I had been asleep for over an hour, and when I woke up, even though we were on a back road with no signs for miles, I asked, "How long have we been in Ohio?" You can tell by the trees, I insisted, but that wasn't it, really. I knew it before I even opened my eyes, knew by the particular warmth of the sun through the windshield, knew by the distinct rustle of wind, knew by the cool mud weight of Ohio air on my heart. It didn't much matter if it was Oberlin, Batavia, Logan, Athens or Columbus—it all felt like something so familiar I could fill my lungs with it. It was dangerous, really, how the air soaked into my lungs, because sometimes, it's easy to forget that breathing out is just as important as breathing in.

∼℘∼

It was just so damn hard to hate Billy Inmon. He was a bastard, a complete bastard, but a quaint one, an unassuming one. He was living in a tent and he was hungry. He was just so hard to hate.

Not to say that we didn't try. Not to say that he didn't sometimes step over that line. Eighteen days into the strike, a young activist pissed on Inmon's tent, a protest of his anti-gay policies. That's when Inmon came out of the tent with a gun. No one got hurt, of course, but we were getting nervous. We all already knew he was pro-gun and anti-gay. We just didn't want to think about these things in the same sound bite. We didn't want to think too hard at all. He was, after all, just standing up for what he believes in, he was just a man with principles. We all wanted so much to hate him.

∼ℯ∼

I first met Claris at Bernie's, the campus bar I had been going to since I was sixteen, where punk bands and aimless artists made their home. Claris, with spiked hair and fake fur coats, Claris with leopard skin boots and an affection for small reptiles: good old eccentric, crazy Claris. Claris was all eyes, and she horrified me, the way she could carve me out of context with her black, scorching eyes. I learned not to talk to Claris, just listen. "You keep listening to her and she'll scare the shit out of you," her friend Marie would tell me. And it was the truth.

Bernie's specializes in gaudy, thick-painted canvases hung by strapping cable from its low basement ceilings. That August, Claris had her paintings on the walls. There were never tags to label the art, but I witnessed Claris hanging them early on a Sunday afternoon.

I wandered toward one of her dark, choppy portraits. "Is this yours?" I asked.

"How should I know?" she said, her boots clopping past me on the cement floor. "I just paint them. It doesn't matter who owns them. Why? Does it look like something I should own?"

The facial expression was jagged and unhappy, the eyes empty and lost. "It looks like you," I said.

"No," she said. "It looks like you."

～

Back to home, for the last time, the place where I couldn't, simply wouldn't return. The dirty yellow house which is next door to Reverend Phillips with the sunflowers planted out front, which is next door to a crack house, which is one door down from the corner of 12th and Jefferson, where they sit on the corner and call "hey baby" to every woman who walks by. But back to the dirty yellow house, and my mother's four latest cats with various ailments and schizophrenias over whom my mother fusses day in and day out. Back to my mother: my poor, crazy mother.

That summer, my mother was shorter than me for the first time. She was always five foot nine, well over an inch taller than me, and even though I had not grown since the eleventh grade, she was hunched and small, hunched and weak, and I felt like I towered over her frail body.

The house was always in some bizarre order, an arrangement of dead plants and bibles, bills and family photos, and of course, empty tea cups. My mother spent her days drinking cup after cup of tea, so the kettle was always whistling in this house, sometimes for hours at a time until my sister or I would come home to turn it off. She wouldn't always hear it. She would be praying: mumbling and shuffling from room to room, raising her hand up without warning, her brow furrowed with worry lines. I never knew what she prayed for. But I knew what I prayed for. I wasn't about to give in to the god my mother had, but I sure tried for faith, for faith that my mother would find a day when she didn't scream at the demons in her house, didn't slam kitchens pots together, didn't hear voices that made her cry for God to help her, to save her from this disheveled and lonely life.

My mother kept the television on most of the summer, whether she was watching it or not, and she told nonsensical moralistic stories with blurry connections to made-for-TV movies, tabloid news, and the latest episode of *In the Heat of the Night*. We were eating dinner in front of the television one night when the news came on, and there he was, twenty-one days into the strike, and it seemed like there was so little left of him. My mother dropped her fork on her plate, a spasm running through her body. She turned off the TV and began to pray.

Claris acquired a video camera during the last week of Inmon's unsuccessful hunger strike. At this point, convinced the man was on his death bed, she went on something of a pilgrimage to talk to him, to chronicle what she thought would be his final days. Claris, with a purse full of psychotropic medicine and Cuban cigars, had a strange new hero in Inmon.

She arrived with flowers, Easter lilies. His face was sallow and thin, bags under his eyes drooped all the way down to meet up with the wrinkles around his narrow lips. He stared at the flowers for a long time, didn't know what to do with them, passed them from hand to hand, all the while shifting around on his lawn chair.

Claris rambled into the camera, an invisible narrator, the camera focusing on the paste-colored flowers, on Inmon's paste-colored face. "I am here today with a man who has sacrificed his place in the world for a cause he believes in. This man should serve as an inspiration to us all." Inmon looked over his shoulder, he looked past the camera, he was losing focus.

The camera wouldn't focus, it wouldn't stay still. Claris was an amateur with a camera, but she knew death intimately, knew it like the back of her hand, as they say. But it's her wrists that told the whole story, pink and shiny, little satin pillows that puckered at the edges like lips ready for a kiss.

"Do you feel death approaching?" she wanted to know, but he pretended not to know what she meant. Actually, he may *not* have known, may have been too busy hoping for someone to interrupt this interview, some radio personality with omelets, perhaps. He smiled self-consciously at her, a bright and stupid grin, pretended she wasn't expecting an answer.

She already had another question, anyway. "What does it feel like to be a martyr, Mr. Inmon?" she asked. It didn't matter to her that he was not dead yet, didn't matter how harmful or hateful his cause. In this moment, it didn't matter that in three days he would finally pass out and be carted off to the hospital where the IVs would replenish him, didn't matter that Voinovich still wouldn't debate him, that Voinovich, in fact, would be reelected by a landslide, all as if none of this had ever happened, as if Inmon was nothing more than a fly buzzing into a microphone at a press conference. By November this was all forgotten, swept under an expensive state house rug. But at this moment, it was still the summer of Billy Inmon. This was the summer when this hunger began to gnaw at all of us, when that question, some important question, began to creep into the darker corners of our minds, made us itch to get out. At least in Columbus, Ohio, that city formerly known as home.

~ℯ~

A Lesbian Homebody

"You have admirable qualities," writes Lou in her last letter to me, "like being affectionate and generous. I feel downright rotten for not loving you." Then she breaks into the language of social workers which, she must know, sets my teeth aching. This woman writing to me, this woman who usually talks with her hands and laughs in rising wheezes, is reaching into her bag of trained vocabulary. I read words like *issues, voice, process*. Reading with one eye, I get a sinking feeling. I see phrases like *take care of myself, come to terms with*, and *evolve into* and know we have reached the end of some little road. Too bad I had already begun the secret task of moving Lou into my home. I am a nester with unquenchable desire for another mature body in the nest. A thirty-five-year-old mother of a six- and a nine-year-old, I keep hoping to figure out a solid approach to making a home.

The home I have as I write this, the "here and now" scratching at the door, often prevents me from writing. I am a single mother doing the single mother jig between teaching, writing, making meals, mediating my kids' disputes, and loving. I leap between surprises of plans gone haywire because of a sick child or storm or friend in need of help. If I stop for a moment and hold my breath, I can hear the whine of the cat, the clump-clump-clump of dress up shoes, a ball bouncing, a UPS truck honking, some kid yelling "you, you, you," and the wind blowing up more unpredictable weather. There are days when this is enough. There are other days when an unnamed longing—for my childhood home, for connection and stability—makes the present seem, at best, tenuous. Only in glimpses, when I am not looking, does the picture of the home I seek shake clear.

∽

I used to know what a home was, when I was twenty years younger and sat in the VW bus with my mother, father, sister, and a gaggle of my father's radical students. Home had something to do with the comings and goings of people. Home also had to do with stories. In my memories we are usually headed some place: to an orchard, a friend's house, a protest. There were often political arguments and my mother took it as her job to protect and interpret for my sister and me. She swam around us, a mermaid, explaining words like *napalm, reconnaissance, Black Panthers,* or other times distracting us with her childhood stories which were set in a time when the idea of "wrong" was as concrete as our national wrongs in the '60s.

One of her stories I remember was about a twelve-year-old kid named Dickey Diangelou. He had a fierce crush on my twelve-year-old mother. He and my mother grew up on the rough side of the tracks in Pittsfield, Massachusetts. One winter afternoon, Dickey, my mother, and a good part of the rest of the neighborhood went ice skating. My mother ended up flat on the ice after Dickey Diangelou punched her in the head, a mittened fist to her pretty face. A bunch of girls pulled my mother home on a sled thinking she might be dead or at least in a coma. My mother finally came to and when she did, she was angry—wouldn't talk to Dickey, not one word, all that long winter. The next spring he showed up at her door, a huge branch of grape lilacs blooming in his arms. My mother told us how some things should not be forgotten. She told us how she took the lilacs back into the kitchen then returned to the door to send Dickey away. I can imagine my mother waving her hand like a queen saying "shoo." I can see Dickey trudging home, long-faced and droopy.

The stories my mother told us were often about toughness: the one about her summers life guarding—saving two girls at once from Pontoosuc Lake. Or there's the story where she told her aggressive French professor to "stay the heck off her back" because she had just received news of her own mother's failing health.

My earliest sense of home includes an image of myself as a listener, a critic. My sister and I were allowed to stay aloof and ask questions. I also remember the more intangible smells of Midwestern shade and woods. A breeze moved through the house which was pre-fab and thin-walled. Our neighbors were other faculty, our closest ones intellectual, Jewish, urban and very loud in the small town of white Protestant conservatives. Sometimes these neighbors would stand in our kitchen with coffee arguing with my father and each other until my mother sent them home. Our home extended into our neighbor's unruly one and out into the ravines and woods, considered safe for kids to roam.

Vines, low branches, deer paths, and shallow streams kept us moving. My best friend preferred to stay inside and watch "I Dream of Jeannie," and "Bewitched," but some days I convinced her to follow me through the woods. I know for a fact that the woods were less safe than we all imagined at that time but somehow our tongues weren't articulate about the dangers children are schooled in now. Rape with a Coke bottle or unwelcome fingers in another ten year old girl were our experiences long before we had the public ability to express them. Vigilance kept us from harm more often than not.

~

I am sure Lou and I have had nothing resembling an argument in the whole year we've known each other. She is laughing her rising-wheeze-laugh at the sight of the refrigerator draining gray puddles on the floor. We tip-toe around each other in the kitchen, two women of slight build. She is Italian, her veins thin blue beneath soft skin. Our requests sound awkward. "Would you mind, when you get a chance, taking a look at the fridge," I ask her. "Would you keep the kids back," she says as she swings into action. I mop, apologize, and keep the kids back. Maybe my idea of home includes finding a woman who can fix refrigerators.

She brings cupcakes and watercolor paints for my son and daughter even though I know from her lifted eyebrows and conspicuously sealed lips that she thinks I spoil them. I have meals prepared and drinks mixed in the blender two hours before she arrives for the weekend. A mother has to plan if she hopes to make a home. I leave my office, my students, an enormous pile of ungraded papers in time to pick up food, movies, and booze. I let the kids watch extra television while I pull the house into order.

I am flying because every move counts. Sheets come off first and then I go out to the yard to find some flowers. The water is still running in the sink because I started to wash something—the dishes, my feet, the kid's shoelaces—I can't remember what. I am in a frenzy of preparation. Home is a ton of work.

~

My son gets off the bus from school with a drawing called "MY DREAM HOME." I brace myself against the kitchen table. There are two wobbly houses that look straight out of Dr. Seuss, connected by a swinging bridge. Under the bridge two big toothy horses smile. My son likes to draw horses. I think I know what he is about to tell me— that the houses are the exact same size and one is for his dad and his family and the other one is for us. I don't think I could live in my son's dream home. I know he longs for the connections he knew for the first four years of his life. Today I don't have it in me to tell my son that having a home can mean leaving someone out. Hanging my son's picture on the fridge, I tell him I think he might be an artist.

~e~

My kids and I are at the dinner table playing family with Lou. My daughter is on my lap and my son is leaning against Lou's shoulder. Lou sits stiff in her chair. My son sighs as he takes his last bites of ice cream sandwich. It is Sunday evening and Lou needs to get ready to begin the two hour drive back to the city where she will meet her "friend" for a work meeting, she says. For the last ten minutes Lou has been trying to educate me in language over the kids' heads about the realities of gay life. She has been out "in the life" fifteen years to my two years. She is playing the role of cultural anthropologist, talking about heterosexist, hegemonic expectations, the tyranny of mono-gamy, the laziness of gays who mimic patriarchal constructs. She laughs periodically at her multisyllabic insight. I think she believes she is being tactful about the fact that she has a date later this evening.

She mentioned earlier in the weekend that I ought to feel free to see other women. Little nervous red spots appear like hickies on her neck.

When Lou comes out of the bathroom after flossing and using my mint mouthwash, the kids and I walk her to her car out back. I look down and notice that my daughter has fashioned a crust of French bread into a kind of shark's jaw. She is trying to bite Lou on the whitest part of her inner thigh. "You little—" I hear Lou stop herself.

Lou rolls down her window before backing out. "I feel like the family is escorting me out of prison," she says. I laugh and wave like the sport I truly am. I should be saying, "Shoo!" but I give a thumbs up when Lou yells, "Talk to you soon!"

~

I begin to notice that my kids and I are almost achieving what I would call a home. This surprises me. During the week, we could pass for any suburban family full of the push and pull of school schedules, homework, baths, and the rituals of bedtime. I pull my hair out over my son's math problems, then read a few stories that nearly put me to sleep. We have a sense of order and purpose. It is clear, most days, that I know what I am doing.

After dinner, my son and I hold conversations while my daughter runs in and out of the kitchen making small requests and messes with her leftover food. My son wants to know when Lou is coming back and if she is ever going to stay for more than a weekend. "Probably not," I tell him. He shrugs, says he wishes I were still married. Then we move on to cover topics including: nuns, priests, teen marriage, wet dreams, and the environmental costs of growing bananas in Central America. My head is spinning as I scrape the plates.

On the weekends an outsider might be struck by the visual changes in the house. Any number of people might be present. On a large calendar I have written down the plan for who will supervise: grandparents, the kids' father and his Costa Rican wife, or me with a girlfriend like Lou, for example. Making a home feels a little like juggling eggs. There are two eggs in the air even as I write this.

∼

I am unpacking her suitcases and boxes in my dream. Against my better judgment, I am hanging up her clothes in half of my closet. Lou is a drafter and works on a slanted table like the roof of our home. I see her in the living room drawing late into the night, long after the kids and I have gone to sleep.

She simply wants out. Her letter is downright dispassionate with its careless diction. "I could take or leave this thing," she writes. She supposes she is "neutral/ambivalent" about me. I consider the fact that she sounds incredibly bored. What I think next is a grotesque leap.

I once was married to a biologist who had a colleague with a parasitic heartworm. This man hated the heartworm like a person hates their worst relative. One day it molted, outgrew its human home, came right through the hairy chest in a regular science fiction drama. The man held a grudge because of the scar. Many years later, the coiled specimen still decorated the center of his laboratory.

I am no heartworm. With this woman, I have even suggested leaving the heart out of it: big lie. Maybe I was considering home as a mechanical operation or perhaps I was feeling brave at the moment, thinking I'd do anything to hold the life within her one-hundred-and-twelve-pound body, more supple than a herd of elephants, more muscular than a pack of tigers. In bed, after drinking more than a couple shots, she speaks some mysterious language, not Italian. Sometimes she even kisses me on the forehead late at night and I assume that means she likes me a lot. Maybe you can make a home with "liking a lot," I think.

"Well, one of us has to be the heavy," she says, "and it isn't fun." This is how she fields my pathetic follow-up-to-the-break-up-letter-phone-call when I finally get through to her after three tries. My brain feels like one of those sluggish recordings of a car before it hits the concrete wall in the Indianapolis Five Hundred. I can see myself wobbling, skidding, sending up bits of rubber and smoke. Words aren't coming out of my mouth even though I know I have some last bright message to convey. But she is hitting hard with metaphors now: "dead horses" and "sinking ships," and "women like you who expect the moon." I am sniffling. This miserable call will cost me six dollars and sixty-four cents, the cost of half of a pizza or almost enough for a night at the movies, alone. Making a good home requires thriftiness.

"Someone here has to be the heavy," I say sternly to my kids at bedtime when they are throwing pillows at each other and laughing at the top of their lungs. I say in my toughest butch voice, "Cut it out!" They laugh at me. My son tells me to get some sleep.

~e~

I think about visiting the ocean. I remember standing on the rocks with my girlhood friend and yelling "leap." We both would crouch down and shoot across the tide pool as if our lives depended upon it. I would like to take my kids back there, to that time when, sitting out of the wind in the belly of Bulldog Rock, I didn't worry about the tide because I knew I could swim. I would like to spit down in the water to watch the white cluster expand its small galaxy.

I remember, as a child, summer coming through the screens and underneath the sheets where my sister, my best friend, and I slept in one room. Out the window, it was difficult to distinguish the fireflies from the stars as my eyes blinked involuntarily in the heavy dark. If I stayed awake long enough, I could hear my parents talking in bed. They whispered and laughed together. Their voices headed some place but then they stopped. A little later, their voices and quiet laughing began again. This went on for as long as I can remember.

~❧~

Mornings I fix breakfast before I am awake. My kids stuff their bag lunches in their packs, push each other to be the first out the door. They are off in the big yellow bus that wobbles beneath the wave of the driver who has such long sideburns, they almost kiss at his chin.

I come back to myself after several cups of coffee. I recognize my brain which is working at its reliable capacity. "Take your head out of the blender and wipe the marinara from your eyes," I say. I am not the kind of person who says things like this.

So here I am. This is our home. I pull myself up by my bootstraps which only means I throw a heap of the kids' clothes in the wash and try to resume life among the kid-shuttlers of the suburbs. Our neighborhood goes like this: lawn, lawn, pit bull, lawn. Some lawns have signs that tell you about their toxic chemicals. There are two pit bulls who lunge at the wire when the kids and I walk along their side of the street. I live here, a low-profile lesbian, and wait for the school bus every day.

I am bold at the beginning. You could even call me fearless—my heart pressed right there near her heart, my thigh moving whatever rhythm is in the air around us. Home waits behind me where my children's drawings fill the kitchen. Home is the stories that help us learn our lives.

MONALESIA EARLE

~e~

The Black Bead

*Even in the yeasty madness of New York, the idea of home beats
in the breast of every living thing. Home is about dreams and community and giving and taking. It's about leaving things behind and
coming back for them later. But most importantly, home is about
the ability to remember.*

My mother sits alone in her ground floor apartment, waiting for one
of her children to come home and keep her company. She does not
care which child it is, as long as it is one who fills up space. Colors it.
Collects it like moss on the side of a tree.

The window she looks out of all day, every day, is covered with
the film of her unnamed longing. It's useless to wash the panes,
because her longing is too great. It has made the glass fragile, almost

papery thin. I know that someday, the grayness of her misery will shatter it.

The window is eye level to the sidewalk and iron bars are welded to the frame to keep out intruders. Foot traffic moves right past her nose, but she doesn't see it. She doesn't see or feel much of anything these days. Her girth, spread around her middle like comfort, grows larger each time I visit. Almost as if she's collecting sadness for us both. I watch her once thick, wavy hair grow thin and brittle from inattention. The same as my heart does when she stares past me at something just left of my shoulder. She'll look at anything but me, a daughter she no longer knows. A daughter who comes home over and over again, only to be met by a stranger. But come home I do, in my Pavlovian way. Salivating in my quest for love. Tirelessly returning to a place that reeks of forgetfulness.

She is from Virginia, my mother, but that's all I know about her. The high yellow complexion, passed on to me and my sisters, once glowed with health and supple beauty. Now it is sallow and lifeless. My own skin itches in sympathy.

I do not favor her as much as my younger sister does. I'm my father's girl. No mistake about that. I wonder if that's the thing which stands between us. My father, long gone to another woman. Remarried and repopulating the world with the seed of his dark black loins. My face is his. It haunts her nights and tangles up her days with bitterness.

My father is six foot two. The last time I saw him with my mother, her five foot frame was bent like an accordion under the sink, where his wrath had tossed her. Forty years ago, but I remember it like it was yesterday. My mother, sliding across the floor, her head barely missing the tall, cast iron legs which held the kitchen sink aloft.

My memory of that moment is that time stood still, like a silent movie reel, stuck on a sprocket, refusing to advance to the twentieth century. My tender mouth formed itself into a shocked moue and urine slowly trickled down my skinny legs. I was rooted to the spot, just like my mother, who was rooted to the hardness of her life.

I wasn't yet tall enough to have to duck as I stumbled slowly toward her, joining her under the sink and praying hard for my small presence to give her comfort. That was the day I came to fear my father for the first time. And he, that man who was squinting so hard at us, as if we belonged to someone else, walked out.

I look at my mother's hands, illuminated now in shadowy wisps of light. They are folded primly in her lap, as if the smallness of that act exonerates her from meeting my gaze. Her coyness cannot disguise the strength in those hands, hard and wrinkled as they are from bearing down and giving us life. Nine of us. My sisters and brothers and half-siblings; for my mother remarried too. Her husband, a good man with bad luck. He worked more than he had to. I think he was weary of coming home to her muteness.

But her hands are never really still. A black bead rolls aimlessly between the spaces of her fingers. Her dexterity is better than ever. The bead appears and disappears, but rarely stops. It's a trick she learned as a young girl. I'd heard that her favorite uncle was a juggler, a card shark, a jack of all trades. In the one picture I've seen of her smiling, it is when he is teaching her how to roll the bead without stopping to think about what she's doing. It's the only picture she pulls from the photo album more than once. When she examines it, she tilts her head back ever so slightly, like she's listening in on the mysteries of the world.

There are no pictures of me. Her new family dominates page after page. My siblings and I are from a past she would just as soon forget. But I can't let her forget, because if I do, the way home will be erased.

My father's side of the family perpetuates a myth about my mother. They say her slanted eyes and her yellow hue comes from Chinamen, but they say it in whispers and real fast, and it makes them sound ignorant. My mother won't set the record straight. Why should she, her eyes accuse. She grew tired of their talk long before I was even born.

I've heard my mother's voice only a few times in my life. A woman who carves the fat off of words, she speaks in punchy non sequiturs. There's a sort of throaty whine that she wraps around her vowels, at once irritating and disconcerting, but useful for the images it evokes. I picture her camped out under the sink, talking a mile a minute.

If I could make her talk now, open up, acknowledge my presence, these are the things we might say:

"Your father and I got married today. Of course, you're not even born yet, but someday you will be, and you need to know these things. Shall I tell you what I wore?"

I am a girl, and when I'm born, I'll be the apple of my father's eye. He will tell the men he works with at the grocery store, that his wife is his loyal companion and that I am the proof of their undying love for each other.

"My dress had a high bodice. You know, the kind with beads along the edges to accent the rise of my breasts. Don't get me wrong. It was a modest dress. I may be poor, but that doesn't mean I wasn't taught how to be a lady."

One of my father's hands is large enough to cover the top of my mother's head. He uses it to lean handsomely against the old dresser his grandmother gave him for a wedding present. His foot, which is too big for ordinary shoes, scratches the back of his muscular calf. His T-shirt is stark white against his black skin. Will I love him as much as he will come to love me?

"Your aunt Winifred was at the wedding. She took a liking to your father, but I met him first. I asked her to be one of my bridesmaids. But, judging by the sour look she had on her face, you would've thought she was at a funeral. I thought she'd be happy meeting your father's middle brother, but she wasn't. I had to apologize to him for her rudeness."

Daddy, throw me high in the air when I'm little, okay? I know you'll catch me and won't let me fall. The sky will be at my fingertips and I'll pick out a star just for you.

"Your father and I had a son. I know you've been waiting to come along, but it seems that that business about carrying a girl high and a boy low, wasn't quite right. But you'll love your brother. He has long fingers, just like your dad. Luckily, he has my temperament."

Daddy, can't you make a little girl? Mommy wants someone she can bake cookies with. A little girl she can teach to dance and laugh and long for her when you don't. I'm ready to come out now, Daddy. May I?

"Another boy. Is it me? I thought for sure I'd be waking up to find you suckling at my breast. There are lots of girls in your father's family. It shouldn't be all that hard to get one out of him. I already know who you are and what your name is, so there's really no need to not have you here."

This man who will be my father, comes home late from work. He is tired and dirty from the boxes he stacks one on top of the other, at the grocery store. Yet, he is very dashing in his weariness. He wears his hair in a wavy pompadour, like the Italian men he admires. He is only twenty-seven, but already a father two times. The other men, the ones he works with, pass out cigars and clap him on the back. His second son will help to carry on the family name.

"It's time for you to learn some lessons in life, Louise. When two people don't get along, there's no sense in them staying together and being miserable. Your father has met someone else and he's gone. We will never speak his name again in this house, do you understand?"

I was born two years ago and my daddy threw me high in the air. I clutched at the stars, but they slipped through my hands. My promise broken, he is gone. I am little, but I am to blame for his leaving.

❧

The light streaming in from the outside grapples silently with the darkness inside my mother's apartment. Shadows grow long on the wall, and the low wattage of the desk lamp works valiantly to keep old secrets at bay. There are tick marks on the living room wall. To anyone whose home is not blessed with children, they simply look like hieroglyphics. But I know it is a place to mark the progress of boys and girls growing as fast as weeds. I touch the one where my brother's head rested, the day he turned five and puffed out his chest to match his delight. The tick marks crawl upward with each precious child. I feel the skin around my mouth tightening, my lips stretching out into a straight, thin line. There are no marks for me. Did I ever exist? I turn to my mother who turns away. The chair she sits in is worn. The fabric faded and threadbare. It has grown fat in the sun, its stuffing coming out in woolly tufts, but she has withered. Or at least her hope has.

I peel myself off the canvas that she prepares for each arrival. Blotches of a presence is all she wants. No solid, tangible thing. Just streaks of movement. Enough to remind her that someone is home. Anyone. Her unseeing eyes and mute tongue erase me faster than I am able to recreate myself. The black bead rolls between her fingers. Never once does she drop it or interrupt its course.

I'm not sure how to reach her. Get inside her head and make her see me. My siblings fare better, but not by much. They tell me to keep coming home, that one day she will remember my name, stop mispronouncing it, calling me Lois. I am too embarrassed to correct her. My own mother who cannot remember my name or the year I was born. I simply take what I can get from her, but it isn't ever all that much. The black bead disappears.

The mole on my mother's chin has sprouted hair. She pulls at it sometimes, like an old man who strokes his beard and contemplates the fate of the world. A persistent and unmistakable popping in her right elbow keeps time with her pulling motion. I am concerned that her arm does not operate to its maximum potential. Was it the sink? The ride she took on the wings of my father's fury? Forty years ago. He could have killed her if he had not been in a hurry to meet his friends at the local tavern. She was saved by his love of beer. That time. There were other times I don't remember as clearly.

She has a bum leg, and when she gets up to use the bathroom, it wobbles around this way and that. Her cane supports her bulk and her good leg works furiously to compensate for the imbalance. She is almost as wide as she is tall, which gives her the appearance of a fat midget, although five feet was an average height for a woman back in the thirties and forties. I watch her eyes move around, but there is no gleam in them to light her way. Her apartment is gloomy, for it has absorbed her personality. Nevertheless, I keep coming back. Like a homing pigeon, I am trained for mindless repetition.

There's no room in her life for me. With each visit, she grows more distant. I touch the walls in hopes that some of who she is will seep into me. Help her recognize that my nose is hers, my lips, the way I crack open a nut with my teeth, suck ice cubes down to a sliver and then spit the wet shards out on the hot pavement. If I rub the years of memories off her walls, she'll have no choice but to call my name. Say it like it's supposed to be said. Let me come home to her. To myself.

∽

"I have to put you in an orphanage. I can't take care of all of you kids by myself. This is your father's doing, not mine. He shouldn't have left me like he did. I'll come for you when I can. The nuns will treat you fairly."

I am only five years old. I do not know what an orphanage is, but I don't think it's a place for little kids. Things are too big here. The clawfoot bathtub in the sterile white bathroom reaches for me when I am ordered to descend into its cavernous belly. I cannot negotiate the rungs of the ladder which takes me to the top bunk where I've been assigned to sleep. My fear of heights carries no sway here. I used to love heights, but I couldn't get a star for my daddy. The other kids whimper at night, when the lights go out, but I do not. I am five years old.

"If you cry, the nuns won't take you. Please be a brave girl. This is a nice place and it's only temporary. Just until I get on my feet."

I understand "only," but not the other word my mother uses, "temporary." I know that she uses the first word when she wants me to wait for something to come to me. "Only for a little while," she says when I'm expecting Santa Claus, but can't figure out the hands on the clock. I go to sleep instead and he's long gone when I wake up in the morning. "It's only Mr. Hall," she tells me when she needs to leave me at the candy store down the street and I scream and kick at the thought of what happens when she's not there. Mr. Hall tells her I'm a good little girl, but I'm not. His hands show me that I'm not. I do not understand "temporary." Is it a more important word than "only?"

"It won't be long. I love you kids, but it's time to go, okay?"

There's a crack in my mother's voice, but I am no longer interested in what she is saying. I link pinkies with my second brother, who is older than me by two years. My little sister, who is too young to walk, is cradled in the arms of a woman who says she's married to God. I wonder to myself if my mother could find someone as good as God to marry. Then she wouldn't have to leave us. The nuns tell my mother that we will be in the same building, but not in the same section. Those are the words I listen to, because they are my new reality. My mother stopped existing for me the moment she said, "Only."

~

I didn't see my mother again until I was fifteen. After six tortuous months in the orphanage, my father's sister rescued us. Her altruism became fodder for all the things she thought was wrong with my parents. By the time I worked up the courage to contact my mother, she had become larger than life, and doubly wicked for abandoning me. But she was the part of me that was missing, the mystery that kept me searching for home.

But as I stand in the middle of her small apartment, my rootlessness finally quelled, I recall all the trips which brought me to her door. Now that she is dead, gone to ashes and dust, I have no trouble seeing her because I've learned to make my own memories, rewrite my past.

I am tall in comparison. My arm is fitted loosely about my mother's shoulder, fingertips toying with the light cotton fabric of her dress. I smile and so does she. It seemed like only moments before that she opened the door to my knocking, welcoming me in as if I were a long lost friend. She desires my company and revels in telling me so. We are friends, best buddies. When she looks at me from under heavy black lashes, I see myself reflected in her eyes. Words tumble out of her. I find it hard to keep up with the history she shares. Who I am. When I was born. Her pride in me. Our home is a place with shimmering colors on taut white canvas.

Our apartment is on Chauncey Street. Your father and I have lived here for six years. I can't tell you how good it is to bring you home from the hospital. You were my easiest birth, you know. Everything went so smoothly. You were born at twelve-oh-one a.m. on Monday, February 5th, 1955. It's a day I'll never forget. The men from your father's job sent me flowers, a nice gesture considering the fact that I only know them well enough to wave from afar.

"Francie's mom said she could spend the night at our house. Will you let us help you bake cookies? Francie likes chocolate chip. She's bringing over her new dolls so we can fix their hair and dress them up in their new outfits."

You have your father's good looks, Louise. Judging by where those pants are hitting you on the leg, I think you're going to be tall just like him. Guess I'll have to buy you some longer ones next time. You already dance like he does, kinda loose-limbed and strange, like you have a melody all your own flowing inside. Makes you seem dreamy sometimes, as if you don't have a care in the world.

"Let's go to the new museum that opened up last week, Mom. I can barely get enough time with you, what with your church activities and all. How about the two of us spending the day together? I'm only home from school 'til next week."

You come from a long line of good strong stock. My side of the family is from Virginia, and your father's side is mostly from the Carolinas. He and I met through a mutual friend. That's how folks did it back then. We had to have introductions and all. Not like you kids do nowadays. I'm the third of ten children. Your father is the fourth of fifteen, but only thirteen of them survived. His side is having a family reunion right around the time of your birthday. Won't that be nice?

"I'm seeing someone, mom. She reminds me of you, except she can't sing to save her life and she's kinda skinny. I think you'll like her as much as I do."

I always knew you were different. I told your father so. I'm sure that's why we love you as much as we do. All of you kids have made your own paths. It's not necessarily the ones I would have chosen for any of you, but when I took my wedding vows with your father, he and I also took vows with each one of you. We promised to stand by you kids through thick or thin, and that hasn't changed one bit. I hope she comes from a good family, that's all.

My mother sits by the window of her apartment. The curtains blow gently in the breeze and the laugher of my brothers and sisters can be heard through the sparkling glass pane. She touches me softly on the hand and searches in her pocket for something she can't seem to find. After a moment or two, she pulls out a black bead. My father walks in and snaps a picture of my mother teaching me how to roll the bead without stopping to think what it is I'm doing.

ELAINE BEALE

∼℮∼

Home⁄ick

I ran away from home at least ten times before I reached the age of twelve. I never ran far. In the small Yorkshire town that I grew up in, there really weren't that many places to go. I remember sitting, a battered cardboard suitcase across my lap, under the wooden bridge that spanned the river less than a half mile from my house. I watched rain splatter down across the murky green water, smelled the dank scent of earth, shivered as the chill of evening leached through my thin cotton anorak, and listened, hard, for the sound of my mother's footsteps on the bridge. Sometimes she came, sometimes she did not. When she did, she would call me, her voice a lilting cry among the whispering, wind-driven trees. "Elaine, are you there, love? Come on, I know you're down there. Come on, come home." And I'd sit there, silent, wanting her to scramble down the muddy, slippery bank, to pull me into her arms and carry me back. Like they did in the films, the hero come to rescue the heroine, the parent come to protect the child.

But she didn't come to get me. She stayed there on the bridge and I could hear her feet shifting impatiently, dull muffled thuds on the wood. "Come on now. You know I'm sorry. I only lost my temper, that's all." I'd push my suitcase aside and pull my knees right up to my chest. Hugging myself and watching the beautiful pattern of the raindrops on the water, like a mesmerizing spell. "Come on, Elaine." I noticed the way her voice got testy. She didn't like to stand out in the rain. "What are you going to do, stay out here all night? You'll catch your death of cold." I heard her start to move away. And then I'd unfurl my body, stand carefully so as not to bang my already aching head on the planks of the bridge, pick up my suitcase and clamber up the bank. I remember the way the wet clay earth felt cold and solid against my palms, the way the suitcase banged heavily against my thighs. When I reached the top, she stood there, arms folded, a clear plastic rain scarf pressing down on her springy hair. "I'm tired of your bloody shenanigans, miss," she'd say and then she'd turn, march away in front of me so I could follow her home.

We moved to a new house when I was six. I never liked it with its bland square rooms, formica furniture and tiny patch of lawn in the back. My father spent hours tending and pruning the roses, planting tidy rows of pansies and garish chrysanthemums. When my mother wasn't working in the hospital she was cooking or cleaning. You couldn't put a book down without it being put away. My sister and I shared a bedroom, which we paced out and staked an imaginary line down the middle. I made her give me money if she wanted to come into my side. I had one shelf above my bed where I could keep my things. I'd started to write a diary when I was eleven. An aunt had given it to me for Christmas, and it had a lock with a little silver key. One day I came home and the diary had been broken open. I remember finding it, the white pages splayed wide as it lay there on my bed. "Why did you do it?" I asked my mother, my hands clenching and unclenching into hard, tight fists.

She scarcely looked up at me from her baking. "There'll be no dirty little secrets in my house, thank you very much."

I loved the fields and the trees and the overgrown lanes of the village. I even loved the way it was so flat that the earth seemed swallowed by the sky. I loved the smell of lilac in the springtime, the days that lasted almost until midnight all through June. I loved picking pounds and pounds of blackberries at the end of summer, my fingers stained purple so you could see the whorls on my skin. I loved the den we built in the junkyard from corrugated iron, the ghost stories we told one another there when it started to get dark. I loved my best friend Carol and my Uncle Roger. I loved my granddad and grandma, the slow, metallic sound of their words.

"Ooh, it's grand to see you," grandma said, pulling me into her sweet and flowery smell. She wrapped her soft, broad arms around me and planted kisses on my head. "Make yourself at 'ome, love. You want some cake? Want a nice cup of tea?" I remember sitting in her springy rocking chair, relishing the chaos of the books and magazines that stood on the floor in tilting piles, the mismatched furniture, the knick-knacks on the fireplace, the cuckoo clock that coo-cooed the hour. I remember granddad playing the banjo, his feet tapping on the carpet, his glossy white hair swept away from his face. I remember eating hard-boiled sweets and peanut brittle. I remember never, ever wanting to leave.

I didn't hear the word lesbian until I was a teenager. It was something the boys called you when they were trying to make you mad. "Lesbie friends," they'd sneer if they saw you walking arm-in-arm with your girl friends or if you'd turned down one of them for a date. Someone once told me that Pete Horner's sister was a lesbian. They lived on the council estate and sometimes I'd take the dog for a walk over there after school. I only saw her a couple of times, and only from a distance, but she didn't look much different from anyone else to me.

I knew I had to leave. Through the evenings spent in front of the local chip shop, smoking so we looked like nothing more than dancing orange circles of light. Through Saturday night discos in the musty village hall, leaning against the wall in one of the dark corners, letting some boy grope clumsily under my shirt. Through Sunday afternoons doing my homework, listening to my parents scream at each other in the sitting room below. Leaving was what I lived for as a teenager.

One night, with Andrew Billany, I stole a bottle of gin from the Off License. I sneaked it out under my jacket while he bought a packet of crisps. We walked to the back of the school playing fields, lay down and stared up at the stars while we got completely and utterly drunk. He told me he was gay. I told him I was, too. And I felt my body sink, like a stone through quicksand, deeper and deeper into the ground. "Do you think we'll meet other gay people?" I asked, my voice a long, slow, distant slur.

"Probably, but we'll have to get out of this bloody dump."

My father had a job that meant he had to go down to London every few weeks. While he was gone he sent us bright and glossy postcards of all the places you read about in books—Tower Bridge, Buckingham Palace, the neon lights in Picadilly Circus. It seemed so big and busy and exciting. It was somewhere you could get lost. I'd only been there once—on a shopping trip with my friend Ann and her mum. We'd taken the train to Kings Cross, but we hadn't been able to work out how to use the ticket machines on the tube, so we'd walked all the way to Oxford Street and back. We gaped wide-eyed at punks with safety pins in their noses, Indian women in embroidered saris, skinheads with their heads shaved smooth as stone.

When I was seventeen, I got accepted at the University of London. I had all my bags packed three weeks before I was due to leave.

The college was in an Afro-Caribbean neighborhood; I'd never seen so many black people before in my life. The woman who ran the student halls of residence said we should be "extra careful" if we went out at night. Almost all the students were white and upper-middle-class. I'd read stories about them in books by Rudyard Kipling and Enid Blyton, but I never really thought I'd come across them in the flesh. When they talked their lips barely moved, as if they were afraid their faces might crack. When they heard me speak, they'd giggle quietly, roll their eyes and cover their mouths with their hands. "Does *everyone* talk like that where you come from?" they asked, as if I was speaking the garbled language of tongues.

I made friends with Darlene, a Barbadian woman on my course whose father worked for British Rail. She introduced me to reggae and took me to the markets in Deptford and Brick Lane. The rest of my friends were women with investment banker fathers. They lived in big detached houses in Kingston-upon-Thames, and their mothers had "domestics" in to clean twice a week. I changed my accent, I learned to fit in. And I looked around the coffee bar, the halls of residence, the freshman ball, trying to spot the lesbians.

And then I found them. In riotous, screaming dyke hordes. I started going to feminist meetings where they'd plan subversion of the patriarchy. I went on marches, laughed and sang songs and taunted the police. I fell, head over heels, in love. I moved into a squat with five other dykes and we started to build our communal, male-energy-free home. I learned to plaster and glaze and install the plumbing. We hung a new front door, which we painted Suffragette purple and green. We never got the hot water installed; I had to visit friends if I wanted to take a bath. When I woke on winter mornings, the first thing I saw was my breath. Drafts ran through the house like gales, and mold grew like an explorer's map across my bedroom wall. But it was all right because we were all in it together. And it didn't really bother me when they laughed at the ragged remnants of my northern accent, or at my mother's nervousness when one of them answered the phone; that they gave me nicknames that I never liked, or that two of them had money set aside in trust funds, but somehow they couldn't spend it on the house. I lived there until I finished my degree. Until everyone had fallen out, made up, slept with someone else's girlfriend, and fallen out again.

I remember sitting in meetings, alongside women with PhDs and double-barreled surnames. I remember how they all seemed so articulate, how I nodded and listened and never said a word. They said they weren't sure how they felt about masturbation, and if you liked penetration it was identification with the enemy. They ate vegetables I'd never heard of, and bought three story houses in Hackney for themselves, their lovers, and their cats. They talked about sexism being the primary oppression and most of them never seemed able to remember my name.

Gina was different. We met at a conference and when I heard her speak, I moved immediately across the room towards her. She came from where I'd come from. She talked the way I'd talked. She used the same phrases my grandma had, she swore just like my mother. Her father was a docker, her mother worked as a cleaner in a nursing home. She drank hard like my father, she told dirty jokes and laughed loud with her head thrown back, just like all my aunts. And she was contemptuous of all the academics, the nice girls who'd gone to Oxford, the women with the BBC accents. "Nowt but a bunch of middle class gits," she'd announce, glancing round the party we'd just crashed. She was family, she was home. In more ways than I'd bargained for.

It happened slowly, in incremental inches, the change from bright romance to fear. At first I'd just sit dazed by a nasty comment, or a lie she told me that she insisted was true. I don't remember the first time she screamed at me or the first time she yelled and yelled and yelled. The first time she kept me up all night and wouldn't let me sleep. The first time she slapped me. Or the first time she hit me with her fist. I do remember when she promised, at a party, that she would break my nose. Or the time she ripped my new, expensive T-shirt right off my body, and I stood there shivering as the goose bumps rose across my chest. And I remember that night, on the way home from the pub, how she pushed me into grayed, slushy snow and I crouched on my knees and begged her to stop. "Shut the fuck up, can't you? I've had enough of your bloody crying, for God's sake." And just like I had as a child, I began to run away.

It took me months to break free. From my lover. From my friends. From the people who'd done nothing when she'd raised her hand and I'd flinched and backed away. I moved to the other side of London, into a beautiful but run-down Georgian house. And to take my mind off my nervousness, the nightmares, I threw myself into making a new home. The two women I shared with and I repaired the walls, painted the interior, built kitchen cabinets, refinished the floors. We were almost done when we were evicted. We moved to another run-down place that stayed that way because we didn't have the energy to do it all over again.

Lisa was from the United States. She was sweet and kind and she said that she loved me. And I wasn't sure, but I thought I loved her back. She asked me to move with her to California. I said yes because I wanted to be somewhere sunny and foreign and different. I wanted to travel and see the world. I wanted to go somewhere no one would know me. I wanted to leave the pain of home behind.

I remember driving from the airport, moving in a flood of big American cars. And I felt like I was living in a movie, gazing from the Bay Bridge across the water to Alcatraz island and the Golden Gate. Lisa had rented a little pink stucco house in Oakland and I remember pushing open the door, taking off my shoes and letting my feet sink into the warm pile carpet as I walked from room to room. She said she wanted to spend her life with me. I lay back on the big soft sofa and let her words flow over me like a song.

I was homesick for months. I missed everything, even the weather. I couldn't get used to the arid landscape, the low-lying morning fog, the absence of clouds in the big blue sky. I often couldn't understand people, they often couldn't understand me. I didn't know which bus to take, what time the last BART train left, and I'd never learned to drive. People thought I was being cold when I was trying to be friendly, they thought I was rude when I was making a joke. The chocolate tasted like it was made of wax, and no one knew how to make a decent cup of tea.

But I loved driving to the ocean. The bright, sparkling, cold white waves of the Pacific. The fine, flat sand. The tiny birds that ran in crowds along the shore. I loved the redwood groves and the smell of pine when we took a trip to the Sierras. The massive open spaces in the mountains with nothing but trees and rivers and rocks. I loved the sunny days of October, heat rising in waves off the freeway while back in England I knew it would be bleak and cold and damp. And I remember the awe of walking through the Mission, into the Castro, all those lesbians, gay men. All those queers. I held hands with Lisa and for the first time I didn't give a damn.

We broke up five years later. I moved out, into my own apartment. I bought a toaster and a bed. I renewed my British passport and bought a round-trip ticket to Heathrow. I wanted to test the water, to see if I knew now where I belonged.

I remember strolling, jet-lagged, through Portobello Market, inhaling the smell of Jamaica patties, vegetable samosas, curry, and fresh-baked bread. The sound of reggae mixing with Indian sitar which, as I walked further, was overwhelmed by seventies punk. I sat on trains that fled past lush green countryside, stone-hewn churches, long-dead smoke stacks in distant cityscapes. I rediscovered flamboyant turns of phrases, and I drank warm English beer down at the pub. Old friends updated me on gossip. We laughed about all our past mistakes and stayed up drinking tea half the night. I held my grandmother's soft and liver-spotted hand and taped her as she told me the story of her life. I stood outside the house I grew up in; there were new people living there, the woodwork had been painted and they'd put up a new fence.

When I went to visit my parents, my mother greeted me at the door. "Ooh, it's so nice to have you back, it really is, love." She pulled me into a hug as I let my arms hang loose. My father talked to me for twenty minutes before he turned on the television. My mother drank sherry in the evening until her eyes were glazed and wet. "I remember when you were little, how nice things were back then. I miss those days, don't you, darling? I wish we could go back and do it all again." I shrugged and turned to the television, the only source of light in the room.

Nothing was quite the same. There were new pound notes, new coins, and I felt like a foreigner standing in the supermarket fumbling with my change. Shiny, plastic Burger Kings had replaced my favorite greasy spoon cafes. The docks were gone, now new developments with renovated warehouses made into yuppie flats. There were new television shows I'd never seen before. A couple of people asked me if I was Australian, "It's that funny accent, dear."

I flew back to San Francisco, staring out the tiny porthole window as we swept low over the flickering lights all around the bay. I walked dazed into the airport, searching the expectant faces for my friends. When I woke the next morning, I drove down to the beach. The sky was polished blue, and the sand glittered in the sun. I walked along the shoreline, letting the icy cold water lap over my feet. And I watched a slow, gray ship move toward the horizon, then, following the curve of the earth, sink silently away. I picked up a handful of pebbles, held their smooth heaviness in my hand, tossed them so they arced high then fell, scattered in the waves.

VALERIE MINER

~e~

Holding On to the Day

At five-thirty this warm afternoon, the crows circle low for last bugs. Golden waves of grass shimmer down hills to the pond. It's been a quiet day. Our hammers. The planes. Otherwise, you have to listen closely to hear wind scratching through dry grass, crickets twittering, the woodpecker tapping in a straggle-limbed oak, the call of roosters, simmer of blessed yellow-jackets. Simmering at a maddening pitch, the pot never quite up to boiling, still threatening to spill any moment. As I watch the sun shredding magenta clouds, a single deer prances from the redwood grove to graze near the pond.

I cherish these sunny winter evenings, remembering the brilliantly naive possibility in today's blue sky. Overcast weather fills me with uneasy pressure. In that greyness, shapes and colors juxtapose, rather than flow through one another, creating an *or* day rather than an *and* day. It's hard to crank up imagination in such a cotton-padded world. No atmosphere for daydreaming, it seems easier to fantasize in sleep. But today has been bright, filled with small successes and mistakes.

I marvel that I'm still in Mendocino—or coming back here—after twelve years. I'm a city girl, a coastal woman, who is gradually, irrevocably, making friends with this land. For the last dozen years my partner and I have been building—sometimes with neighbors and electricity, sometimes by ourselves—a cabin in the hills of Mendocino County. At first, I felt confined by Helen's dreams about these one hundred and sixty acres she owns collectively with twelve others. I didn't even own a house or apartment in the Bay Area—the place where I lived and worked. Why would I want to build a cabin? Meanwhile, Helen and I were also editing a book together. The cabin, which was meant to be a haven, could, in the ensuing tension, pull our lives apart. Now, after visiting Mendocino across the seasons, after our jobs have uprooted us from California, after learning how to tie rebar and shingle a roof, I have strangely come to see this unfinished sixteen by twenty foot cabin as home. Unfinished. Always one more thing to do—the sheetrock, the tiles around the wood stove, the kitchen cabinets—my god, what would we do if it felt complete? No worry, given our pace.

Strange, which days, among so many, come to mind. I recall walking up the hill to our cabin, feeling the three hour drive from

Oakland dripping off my body. By the time we reach the top, the air is cool, the sun half-an-hour to setting. There is our cabin—as we left it—and inside it is warm, holding on to the day for us. The windows are still stacked against the wall. A bed frame lies in pieces at the foot of the old couch Wendy and Kyle found. Joan's borrowed cooker stands on the floor, gasless and rusting near the neatly organized boxes of nails, tubes of caulking, and other future tools. On alternate visits, I am struck by what we have done and what we have left to tackle.

Mendocino mornings are often foggy, but the grey burns away more quickly than it does in Oakland. The cabin is on the crest of a hill and, as we walk out the door, turkey vultures fly across my line of vision. Tiny lizards scurry over our makeshift step. It's hard to recall this as an uncolonized spot of ground. Embarrassing to remember when I was the gringa who hiked a mile down to the highway to wait for the concrete man.

～ั่ะ～

That day, as I walked the long dirt road, I thought about the complex stages of foundation work. We had dug the trenches and pounded the stakes and tied the rebar. Rebar was one area in which I excelled, with my small fingers and steely will. If I ever get hired on a construction crew, I'd be Ms. Rebar. Finally reaching the gate, I cursed myself for not bringing a book because country time was fluid and it could be a long wait. The previous month or year, someone saw a rattler by this gate. What if she were lying in wait now? No, rattlers didn't bother you if you didn't bother them. I knew that. Fifteen minutes passed. Curious drivers slowed down to see if I needed help. Too many other cars came close and fast, for no one expected loiterers on a rural highway. After half an hour, I noticed the vultures over head, circling lower and lower. When I moved a few feet, they lifted themselves in disappointment. After another fifteen minutes, they descended, lower, lower, until I shifted again.

Finally, a heavy old truck appeared and the driver pulled off the highway. Jumping from the cab, he inquired, "What're you pouring?"

"Concrete," I answered uncertainly. What else did he pour from that huge, rusting canister?

"No." He inspected me, him doing the wondering now, about whether he just wasted his time driving from Ukiah. "Are you building a garage? Bathroom?"

"Cabin," I answered curtly. "Can I hop in and direct you to the site?" Site, there was a technical word. Attitude, it's all in your attitude, I told myself. For the rest of the day I summoned authority to my shoulders, non-chalantly raking cement, pretending to understand all the construction lingo.

("What're you pouring?" "Concrete." For weeks, this rang in my ears.)

∽

Perhaps the most exciting stage of building is when the frame is raised on our wall-less cabin. I like to stand in the middle of the skeleton, smelling the Douglas fir, savoring the limitless space, gulping the view, wide open from all four sides. Conversely, I hate making the walls and ceiling, the transition from youth (where all views are possible) to middle-aged compromise. Then again, after we tack up the walls, we get to cut holes in them for windows. And each window admits a new surprise.

Work varies from day to day. One morning I align plywood on the roof and pound in nails along the seams. That afternoon I hammer floorboards, a less rewarding task in the vista and the sense of daring. Fascinating how much I discover about my character when I'm working here. I have zero confidence about obtaining new skills. I assume that if the nail isn't going into the wood, I have the wrong nail or that the wood has changed from last year. It takes a while to know you have to keep trying. Maybe if I hit each nail several times I'll win. I notice that if I aim carefully and proceed with measured strokes, I'm more successful. I add force behind each slam and learn to raise the hammer high enough for a maximum blow so I know when the nail is going in and when I'm wasting my shots. Eventually I become competent. Instinct functions better than will. Invariably it's when I'm concentrating too much that I mess up. Usually hammering is a good break from writing. But tender, newly-discovered muscles in my thumb make it painful to hold the pen.

Some labors are less pleasant than others. One cold night we have to change the privy barrel. I close my nose and think of those Chinese short stories about "night soil" workers. If the stories don't make recycling shit more fun, they at least make it more universal. Occasionally obsessions overwhelm and I know I'm going to be killed. Falling off the ladder is a constant fear. Then the double whammy as I balance on the ladder to tack up trimboard: what if I hit a bat's nest and get bitten by a rabid vampire? Gradually, I learn to be amused by my constant resistance to new tasks and to feel satisfied after a few hours of climbing and measuring and hammering.

Still, I leave most precision work for Helen. The day we install the loft window, Helen and our neighbor Kyle take over. My job is mowing the grounds to keep down fire danger. Since we're over a mile from the highway and there's no fire hose, our cabin could be gone by the time the volunteer fire brigade woke up. Mowing is interesting because in the last month, the grass has gone from moist, green silk to brittle sticks. As I trim the thistle and other vegetation from under the house, I find skillfully dug entrances into the ground, home away from home to the lizards who spend half their lives in our cabin. At the end of the day when the mower and saw are turned

off, we hear a loud chorus from the oak tree behind our house—
birds celebrating that the hill is theirs again for the night.

I'm very conscious of territory here, aware of the different ways
we animals claim space through structure, sound, movement. One
day after work, Helen and I go for a swim. The pond is freezing and
we yell as we hit the water. All around, birds whirr up in irritation or
panic and sail east to what we call the fishing pond. Nowadays the
birds do more fishing here than we do.

The land is crowded with voluble birds in morning and evening.
Afternoon is insect time as the high, yellow grass resonates with crickets, bees, flies. Bats appear at dusk, dropping from eaves outside the
house, swooping across the grass, then speeding back and forth to gain
their bearings. When Helen and her friends bought these acres, the
Anderson Valley seemed remote. Now the main road is lined with
vineyards and wine-tasting chateaux. Worse, interlopers like us have
begun to build in the nearby hills. Yesterday morning the buzz saws
from several miles away were a faint but persistent reminder of neighbors. You're never a full step ahead; you have to make some beleaguered
peace with change. As I watch the birds glide toward the next pond, I
grow more aware of the vanities and liabilities of my material claims.

～●～

We drive to Boonville one afternoon to buy plants. At first the nurs-
ery looks ridiculously miniature compared to the surrounding miles

of farmland. It is a tiny ranch of pine, cedar, daphne, lavender: trees and flowering plants all on the same level. A tall man with a brilliant red beard delightedly introduces us to the various ceanothus, or wild lilac, and a yellow-flowered, almost hibiscus-looking plant. We discuss sun vs shade, native vs non-native, size, width, color and sheen, and he is loving his job. In fact, he says if we want a California Nutmeg we should go to Ukiah. We don't relish the forty-five minute drive to Ukiah. We like this man. We want to complete the task. It is not surprising that when he introduces us to the California Holly, we nod. He savors the Latin name, *Heteromeles arbutifolia.* Then he produces a picture of how it will look when mature. We listen attentively, hoping we can live up to his expectations. He explains that it is also called Toyon. That the "holly" name comes from its red berries and glossy, dark green leaves. That Hollywood got its name from the plant which grew in profusion behind a Southern California housing development in the 1920s. Now, he says, sadly, there is hardly any Toyon left on that eroded hillside. We nod knowingly. You can hear the "tsks" as we bend our necks and we carry the three pots of Hollywood to the car as if they are another kind of seasonal gift.

On the way home, we stop at Jack's Ace Hardware to confer about the correct width of chicken wire to protect our Hollywood from deer. We decide on a two inch wire and a strong binding material. I also pick up a couple of Tootsie Rolls and a juice bar. On the way out, I notice Jack hanging around the cash register. The old man sold his store earlier this year, but can't seem to pull away. Back on the land, we redirect the hose and miraculously, in ten minutes, the windmill is pumping water uphill. After we mark the ideal distance between trees, we start digging, then fill each hole with water to make deeper digging easier. A little fertilizer later and we have three small bushes, Hollywood transplanted to Mendocino.

~

I love going to Jack's—Oreos and chicken and parkas and nails and block ice—all life's necessities and then some. It's a beautiful ride over the golden hills to Philo, past symmetrical fields of grapevines, through the arcades of green trees. I often stop at Gowan's fruit stand for cherries, apricots, raspberries, apples. When I sit on our stoop popping berries into my mouth, I wonder why fruit tastes more authentic in the country, just because it's fresher? One day at Jack's, I pick up one hundred and eighty pounds of cement, four pier blocks, eight pounds of 16d galvanized nails, five pounds of 16d ring shank nails as well as ice and groceries. I decide I must have become a rural femme because I can't pass up the cotton work gloves with the tiny green rubber dots—much nicer than my filthy old pair with the black dots. I am shocked when the cashier wheels out my cart and insists on helping me load the car. It's my skirt, I'm sure. If he had identified me as one of those dykes who live down the highway, he wouldn't have bothered.

I don't leave my writing life behind when I come to the Anderson Valley. I've worked on various stages of six books here. At first the labor is confined to the initial hand-written draft of a story or to checking typescript or proofs. Nothing is more satisfying than sitting in the morning sun on the rim of a hill and reading. Then I graduate to editing hard copy and, finally, with the installation of our solar electricity, to writing and printing on the computer. I recall sitting in the cabin in the summer heat with lizards scurrying around the books I was judging for the *Los Angeles Times* Fiction Prize. I remember taking *Rumors from the Cauldron* into Ukiah to be xeroxed during a trip to do my laundry. Reviewing Western books like John McPhee's *Assembling California* and Joanne Meschery's *Home and Away* becomes all the more pleasurable as I read them in Mendocino during breaks from teaching jobs in faraway states.

Things have changed these last twelve years. Some small adventures have ended. Washing clothes, for instance, has become a little easier. One morning during the early days, I hung my pants over the sawhorse to dry. A mare hungrily nibbled the wet cotton. I put the clothes out of horse reach—on a picnic table—until the wind blew them to the far side of the house. So I anchored the light pieces down with cans of green chili and refried beans. Nowadays that horse has literally moved to other pastures and we have a clothesline tied securely between two oaks at the back of the cabin. Helen and I no longer have to climb to bed in the loft on a shifting ladder because there's one built in. The barrel of water has been taken down from the roof since we plugged our sink into the well. We eventually replaced Joan's gas rings with a small stove.

What comfort will we next introduce? Will our accommodations insulate us from the rhythms of the land? It's dark now as we lie under the opened brown canvas-and-flannel sleeping bag we still use as a blanket. Helen is sound asleep. I close my eyes to find three red-winged blackbirds, then a kite treading air by the western ridge. Too awake yet for dreaming, I creep to a window to watch the Milky Way sprayed generously through the center of a blueblack sky.

TZIVIA GOVER

~e~

These Walls

"Be homesick for me—you who are homeless—let me be your lover, your home and your country."

—RADCLYFFE HALL IN A LETTER TO HER LOVER,

EVGENIA SOULINE

I was off from work that summer afternoon. Everybody was. There was a hurricane watch and the radio announcers warned that it was to be a big one. I remembered making *x*'s out of masking tape across window panes in our cabins at summer camp. Other stray bits of advice roamed through may head, too: take refuge in the bathtub, keep away from glass. Stand in the doorway. No, that was for earthquakes. No matter, I planned on ignoring all of it. My two best friends and I sat in my second-floor apartment watching MTV.

Then the phone rang. It was her, the butch I'd flirted with on the corner of Main two nights before. She'd slouched against the mailbox as if it were the bar in some smoky hideaway. Now Whitney Sheppard was saying over the phone that she'd come by and get me if I'd like, we could wait out the storm at her house. With giddy apologies I left my girlfriends, and under a night sky in the middle of the afternoon, Whit and I drove in her pickup truck over curving country roads, up and up and up into the mountains, to her house.

Her house was not the kind of place you'd necessarily choose as a shelter in a hurricane: the one and a half story cottage sat perched on stilts with no basement to retreat to. Inside, huge panels of sheet rock leaned against unfinished walls. The bathtub served as the kitchen sink and a black plastic hose hung limply where a faucet should be. The outhouse in the yard was functional. The toilet inside was not. She had recently run the electrical wires. The plumbing was next. She was renovating, she explained as she led me upstairs.

The mattress on the floor of the attic loft was the only comfortable place to sit. The winds had died down. This hurricane was a bust. There was even a finger of sunlight poking through the window and pointing across the white sheets where we would spend the rest of that afternoon.

It would be seven years and (on my part) four apartments later before Whit would invite me to make that house our home. In those intervening years she worked on it with another lover. Together they landscaped and painted and tore down and built up. I arrived back on the scene in time for the finishing work. I helped Whit make a pattern with the tiles on the kitchen floor. I picked the pink carpet for the bedroom, and sanded the grout between the stones of the hearth. Mostly, though, I lay on the couch or the bed, reading or sleeping while she worked. The pounding of the hammer and the whir of the power drill made for an oddly comforting lullaby. I even dozed while she ran the electric sander back and forth across the living room floor. No one could sleep through such a noise—but I did, inhaling sawdust like fairy powder. Somehow that dust of creation made me heavy and slow, unable to lift a hammer to help.

Bless this house oh Lord we pray, keep it safe by night and day.
Bless these walls so firm and stout, keeping want and trouble out.
Bless us all that we may be, fit to dwell oh Lord with thee.

—LULLABY

When I was a child my father would take me with him on his rounds. We'd drive in his station wagon that smelled of shavings from the shingles and roofing paper he piled into the rear. He'd take me from house to house. Usually I'd wait in the car while he walked up muddy paths to building sites where he'd try to interest contractors in siding, Anderson windows, and tile.

Those framed houses looked undignified with their gaping doorways and latticed roofs letting rain, snow and sun enter where they shouldn't be allowed to penetrate. Those houses reminded me of skeletons hanging in science labs, not only naked—but naked of flesh. I'd want to avert my eyes even once the walls were up, siding and sheet rock in place. There was still that vacant stare—windows with suppliers' stickers still in place. Worst of all were those bald lawns; muddy mounds of unlandscaped earth.

Those houses were corpses into which spirit had yet to breath life. And they haunted me like ghosts. They confirmed my lack of faith—my inability to believe in Home. Houses, they whispered, were flimsy as old bone.

Home: Place of origin.... An ultimate objective.

—WEBSTERS NEW COLLEGIATE DICTIONARY

I remember watching through the window that first time Whit drove me towards her house. I noted the way we wove through rising hills, past cow pastures and maple sugar farms—but mostly past miles and miles of nothing. ("Nothing?" she'd argue. "Those trees are like the gates to a city where bears, salamanders, frogs, birds, beaver, fox, coyote, mosquito, lichen, woodpecker, deer, moose, chipmunk—all live.")

Of course I had no idea then that this route would one day be my path home. Or maybe I did when I asked, "How much longer?" and Whit replied, "Oh I don't know, another ten minutes maybe," and I felt an ache inside my belly, as if the long invisible chord that stretched between me and town—me and civilization—had been tugged too taut. Maybe that's when I knew we'd get there, but it wouldn't necessarily be quick, or easy.

Still, inexplicably, as soon as I walked through the door, and I've never once told her this, I was taking measurements. In my mind I was picturing how I'd possess these walls, the alterations I'd make. The couch should face the window, the curtains should be lace, the floors stripped and polished.

Some species of fish mate this way: the male builds a nest, swishing his tail in circles on the river bottom, clearing rocks and plants until he creates a ghostly circle of order and calm. The female fish swims past, and if the nest pleases her, she stays. But does she plan to change things? Add a doorway there? Take down that wall to let in the morning sunshine? How many nests does she consider before she chooses?

As it turns out, when I did finally move in, I couldn't call Whit's home mine. Couldn't do it easily. Knowing it was childish, I complained. Suddenly, somehow, finally settling down, I demanded the sea.

~e~

The town on Long Island where I grew up is not exactly a coastal village. Of course it is, I mean it's on the sea. There's a section called The Harbor whose quaint restaurants have decks looking out on the water, where waitresses in red-checked aprons serve lobster roll. But I wasn't acquainted with that part of town. We lived inland, on an island of our own, dense with side streets and neighborhoods, moated by highways and railroad tracks. I only saw the ocean a few times each summer, in the weeks between the end of sleep-away camp and the beginning of school. Beach to me meant Jones or Lido: blanket to blanket coverage so complete that it was possible to walk from parking lot to surf without setting a toe on the sand. I didn't even like swimming in the ocean—there were riptides and undertows and jelly fish. So where did I come off now nestled into a life in the hills of western Massachusetts, pining for the sea as if I'd been raised on sun-bleached shores?

~e~

It was Valentine's Day weekend when we arrived in Portsmouth and checked into a motel that was clean, characterless, and sterile as the suburbs. I headed for the bathroom first, flicked on the orange heat lamp, and filled the tub. I emptied an envelope of Japanese bath salts into the water and watched as it turned a dreamy turquoise. Whit and I soaked, and soaked. I sent her out for pizza—this weekend was her gift to me and I was calling the shots—and we ate in bed. Before we slept I led Whit down the hall where a hot Jacuzzi lay in wait. Submerged, I was in bliss.

This I called mine: this ancient element, void of architecture, in which, gill-less, I am ill-equipped to survive.

The next night we went out for dinner. We watched the winter ocean through the plate glass window at a seafood place with the same fascination with which we watched fire in the wood stove at home. The waiter was oddly alert, crouching between us to take our order, placing napkins under our water glasses, and asking, "Is everything OK?" many more times than was necessary.

"I want to talk about my house," I told Whit. "Talk," she answered. She knew which house: the one I grew up in. The one I still dream about. The one my mother and I moved out of after my parents divorced.

Home to me will always be 436 Pennsylvania Avenue, that Long Island address I can't stop talking about. The house was an impressive edifice with Doric columns in front, a slate terrace in back ringed by flower boxes planted with geraniums. I knew its pipes, its smells, its betrayals, the light it let in and the corners that were always dark.

For Whit I sketched onto a napkin the curve of the circular staircase which had been the showpiece of that house before we lost it. I described the banister, the nook halfway down the stairs in the arc of the C where there was a window and a shelf for a large leafy plant. All through dessert I described the louvered shutters, the stuccoed outside walls, the doorless terraces off the upstairs bedrooms which we stubbornly climbed out windows to reach.

Down, down two twisting flights of stairs there was the basement carpet that reeked of many floods. In one of the honeycomb of underground rooms crouched a broken toilet. Like a fixture in a dream it appears and disappears with memory and imagination.

Even when it was solid in the present tense, this was a dream house, with melting borders. There was the pane in the glass doors off the sun room that my brother once kicked in. Then there was the window that was kicked in and we never knew who did it. A sparrow gnawed its way through the plastic filler next to the air conditioner in my bedroom. Nest straw seeped through onto my radiator, and sometimes I'd see the mother bird's beak poke into my room.

After the divorce, and after my sister and brother left for college, my mother and I moved across town to an apartment. It was an unremarkable duplex on the main drag across from a biker bar. With pots of red and pink flowers my mother dressed up the cement terrace off the kitchen that barely held one beach chair. On hot days we huddled there with a newspaper and tried to ignore the rear wall of the post office that loomed a few yards away.

We told people that we'd moved for the sake of economic stability and independence. But it was more complicated than that. The house turned on me when I lived there nearly alone. It whispered and hissed and taunted me with its empty spaces. I abandoned that house the way an angry lover storms out after a fight—half expecting to be begged back in.

The exile has been long. I pound on the doors and windows. Demand to be let back in. As if I had forgotten the heavy flower box on the back patio, where we always hid the key.

You have taken the place of the entire world, and what more can a writer want who has built a pyramid of writing, than that someone should be able to enter, feel at home, enjoy and inhabit this pyramid.

—ANAIS NIN, IN A LETTER TO JAMES LEO HERLIHY.

One early morning the phone jangled me awake. Holding the receiver—dial tone now, wrong number—I stood looking at the lush green world outside our bedroom window. The sun had rolled the scene out like a memory—or a dream—and I was struck by how beautiful it all was. As if to etch the moment into my mind, a family of wild turkeys emerged from the fringe of trees and paraded across the far edge of our lawn. I heard myself call out to Whit: "Come, look, we live in paradise."

When Whit bought these ten acres, she was twenty-two years old and already knew her heart. Saw this little house—sagging, slipping back into the earth—and sensed its potential. She felt at home in the woods right away, as if the whole outdoors were her comfortable living room. She notices the silver maples that are dying and the hastas that are blooming. One day when I observed that she didn't play any musical instrument, or make sketches or ceramics, and said, "You should do some art," Whit threw up her arms, and countered: "This is my art."

Of course: Art is creation. Our divine imitation. I make rooms from strings of sentences, as if brick by brick. Her structures are more literal.

I say Whit looks sexiest in her tool belt: the heavy, worn leather weighted down with hammers and pliers, and handfuls of nails. I'm sure she thinks it's just some cheap fantasy of mine. But it's also a genuine ache for the promise that if she can build, she can shelter me. That with these heavy tools slung low like ripe plums at her hips, she alone is the god that can keep me safe. That she will put floorboards below and shingles above. That she is capable of keeping me warm. That with her breath saw dust will skitter across wood and be whole.

Whit says I look sexiest at the computer with my glasses on. Her clichéd, librarian fantasy, I know. But what I am doing there, where I go when I enter the blank spaces between lines—what if she could follow me in?

～º～

The thing about the house I grew up in, I tell Whit, is that it was all about edifices. People were impressed by its elegance. It was the good face we put on for the world. Our way of keeping up appearances. Our shield against what was and was not inside. It was, after all, our identity.

When we have visitors to our home now, Whit takes out the photo album in which she has marked the progression of our house. There she is on the roof painting the trim. There she is underneath the floor, repairing a rotting sill. Those are her arms stretched wide in front of the cement septic tank before it was lowered into the earth.

When the chimney needs cleaning Whit clambers onto the roof with a big wire brush attached to a rope and lowers it into our hearth. We've climbed out the second floor windows and sat on the roof to watch satellites. "This is your planet," I've told her. Like the Little Prince, Whit has found a universe in perfect proportion to herself.

But to me, home is still something mysterious, and bigger than either of us; as complicated as a beating heart.

If I look closely will I see what Whit is showing me? That you can build Home, nail by nail? Anywhere? That I don't have to be homesick, always?

ELIZABETH HOWELL

~e~

Writing from the Center

"I can't help wondering how many ways water shapes the body, how the body shapes desire, how desire moves water, how water stirs color, how thought rises from land, how wind polishes thought, how spirit shapes matter, how a stream that carves through rock is shaped by rock."

—GRETEL EHRLICH

On a cold autumn morning my lover and I drive ten miles from our house to what used to be a town on the banks of the Missouri River— now just scattered trailers, fishing shacks, and old farmsteads. Our excuse is in the back seat: two dogs who don't get enough time in the wild. But we come here for each other too. I was born at the confluence of two of the country's biggest rivers: the Missouri and the

Mississippi. They have served as a compass for my crossings. Jill is river born too, where the Willamette and Columbia Rivers flow toward the sea through Portland, Oregon. Neither of us can resist a muddy current and a gravel bar.

Sometimes we follow the dirt road that runs along the riverbank, at the top of a steep, muddy, often flooded embankment where river junk floats up to lodge in the roots of old trees. This morning we choose the old railroad tracks for our walk, away from the harsh sting of a north wind. The gale coming off the water is so cold that I stumble and curse trying to get the dogs out of the car as they pull desperately at their leashes. I can empathize with their urgency. Both Jill and I, two dogs, and two cats have been sharing a small, dark, cramped house, cheap enough for our graduate student budgets. We're all a little stir crazy.

We head south along the old Missouri-Kansas-Texas rail line, now a state park and path for hikers and bicyclists. Soybean fields lie on either side of us, a glowing ochre sea of dried stalks and bean pods. It is past the height of fall glamour but this year I see color with a new eye, a painter's eye, and the landscape is vibrating with subtle hues of salmon, rose fawn, gold, soft blues and the new green of winter wheat.

The fields are a contrast of wet earth and dry vegetation, the ground saturated by recent rains. Beyond the field to our west is the wide river, brown today, flowing wildly through its overly-engineered channel. To the east bluffs rise, carved from a more ancient and gentle waterway, now softened by delicate branches of oak and maple newly bare. Cedar trees emerge from their summer canopy and huddle low against the beds of limestone jutting from the hillside. Further east a small farm lies in the valley between two gently sloping wooded hills.

Cold wind fills my lungs and I feel like I can really breathe for the first time in weeks. The broad expanse of fields is such a relief after many hours hunched in front of my computer. Between our school work and grading papers, Jill and I haven't really talked much lately. We have taken two hours away from our work because we know this walk will calm and renew us, giving us space to talk about more than what we're having for dinner. On this day, we talk about what we really want to be doing with our lives—writing, painting, throwing pots.

The path is bordered by green reeds and dried stalks of dock and milkweed, the stems turned red and pods hanging dry on the vine like small brown birds. Hawks loop out from the bluff over our path and back again. Jill suggests that my nature is hawk nature, to ride current above bluff, suspended in air for sheer pleasure, going nowhere in particular. The dogs are begging to be off the leash so the golden retriever is let go near a wooden bridge. She starts tentatively down a deer path between the field and the creek, looking back at us as if to make sure she has our blessing. Then she breaks into a full run and disappears into soybeans.

We walk on past the farm and pause beneath the bluffs to look up at the small openings in rock; I wonder how big the caves actually are and whether humans or animals have lodged there. The fallen leaves weave a dense pattern up the steep face, a winter blanket for roots and seeds. At the foot of the bluff, I take her hand gently, make sure we're alone, kiss her fingertips. Our dog returns mud-covered, and as we turn back up the path we let the other run. A black poodle doesn't glide across this landscape as poetically as a golden retriever, but he takes his freedom just as seriously.

Clouds move across the sky in a dance of light and shadow and as we look up from talk we are simultaneously struck by a vision—a line of bare white sycamores, their trunks and branches lit ethereally by sunlight momentarily unobscured by passing clouds, glow against the darkened bluff. We stop, staring, taking in this gift, a crescendo of sky and sun and tree glowing exquisitely, then gone. Jill takes my hand, smiles at me, knowing we will both take this moment and savor it. Something magical always happens on our walks here—it is a place of great capacity—for water, rock, ideas.

Turning up the road to the car I see a great blue heron take off from the bank below me and fly low across the water to the opposite shore. Somehow she maneuvers her giant winged body through the currents of air and water, which to my sensibilities should carry her away. As Jill and the dogs continue down the road, I stand and watch as if to guide her safely across. But of course she lives here, in what seems to me a harsh place for such a beautiful and delicate creature. I am sure she has made that crossing many times.

The heron and I share a home. This land, marked by waterways and cattle ranches, tall grass prairie and wetlands, lives in my bones. As oppressive as the Midwest can be, I am finding a way to be at peace here, to salvage those pieces that feed me. I find this landscape incredibly inspiring in its own way. It does not move me on a grand scale, like the New Mexico desert, or the mountains of the Sierra. Rather it is the bloom of purple coneflower at my front stoop, the nighttime whine of coyote pups, the drone of cicadas, or the musky fragrance of decayed leaves that comes on the first cold wind in November. It is the land which brought me home from three thousand miles away.

~

When I was sixteen I attended a poetry workshop at my high school. My otherwise extremely dull and conservative high school participated in a poets-in-the-schools program and my sophomore English teacher picked me to attend the workshop. I was thrilled to be exempted from yet another class discussion of Stephen Crane's *The Red Badge of Courage*. We gathered in a school lounge, perhaps ten of us circled around an unkempt, balding poet who kept starting to light a cigarette before remembering where he was. He seemed uncomfortable with his "official poet" status, and nervously pushed loose strands of his greasy gray hair behind his ears every few minutes. I saw dirt under his nails and his clothes were wrinkled. He slouched, drank black coffee during the talk, spoke slowly, and told me something I have always remembered.

He talked about places, sense of place. He told us that being centered and being aware of one's center was at the heart of writing poetry. He felt that we had an advantage due to our geographic circumstances—we were already centered in geographic terms. Missouri lay at the heart of the country—dead center. We were also very near the meeting of the Missouri and Mississippi Rivers. He wanted us to take advantage of this wealth of grounded energy—to write from our center and to let the power of these ancient rivers and the wisdom of the continent's oldest mountains, the Ozarks, speak through us. It was the first time I heard anyone speak of land in spiritual terms. Suddenly this place where I had felt trapped, landlocked, isolated from all that could possibly spark my creativity, was presented to me as full and rich and waiting to be tapped.

But it was not until years later, living thousands of miles from where I grew up, that I began to yearn for those things uniquely Midwestern. The poet's words faded as I resumed my tortured adolescent existence. I was a captive of cornfields and small minds. I finished high school without a date or a poem to my name. It slowly dawned on me in college that I was a lesbian, and the only way I could imagine really being a lesbian was to get away from the Midwest. I moved around the country for ten years, living on both coasts and spending five years in San Francisco before I could come back.

The longer I was away, the more I dreamed the land. I craved the night air of August, thick and hot with the smell of hay and the sound of locusts. I missed seasons, and the gold-green light of sun moving through sycamore leaves. I missed red gravel and a certain slab of limestone under my grandparent's cedar trees. I missed my mother, my grandparents, those connections deeper than the need for lesbian community and culture as I lived it in California. So I returned to attend graduate school in the same town where I had gone to college, finding a very different life than the one I left. Lesbians are considerably more visible here now than even ten years ago. There is a Lesbian Community Project, active queer campus organizations, lesbian softball and basketball teams in the city leagues, and a local Pride picnic. But it is a very different story in the surrounding rural areas.

In the spring we rented a house deep in the cattle country of rural Missouri, just a few miles from a small farming town, and still close enough to commute to school and work at the University. We both wanted quiet, a garden, more room for the dogs. To say we rented a house is a bit misleading, since the structure was originally built as a weaving school. The weaver has since moved away and now rents out the school. Her father is buried under the oak tree in the front yard, and we fill her many shelves built to hold wool and yarn with our books and pottery.

Our house is somewhat of a landmark in the area—it was built to resemble a nineteenth-century prairie schoolhouse, complete with a bell tower and school bell which can be rung by pulling on a rope that hangs by the front door. It is not inconspicuous. The weaver painted it red, installed skylights, and had the roofing tile attached in a weaving design. She planted only two trees near the house, so it stands in the middle of a pasture taking the wind and sun at full tilt. The windows on the west look out to pasture and pond, soybean fields, and woods beyond.

A road runs alongside the east side of the property where there are few trees and shrubs, so we are completely exposed to passersby. I have the feeling that everyone sees everything we do here. They have watched us haul in dirt, plant our garden, play soccer, fly kites, throw the Frisbee, drink beer, build a dog pen. They probably think we don't have jobs. It is rare to see anyone outside here, except for work. I am certain there is a great deal of speculation about us, and I struggle daily with balancing my love for this place with my fears about the surrounding conservative community.

One day this summer Jill and I came home from a long day of work and a hot commute. After the round of greetings with dogs and cats hungry for our attention, she walked over and punched the button on the answering machine. I was putting on my gardening clothes, when I heard a muffled voice on the tape saying something about being "gay" and then hanging up. The next message was the same voice, only clearer, a teenage girl's voice, maybe two girls', and much giggling, saying, "Are you two lesbians?"

We sat silently under the exposed wooden beams, thinking about how this call happened. I flashed past all the ways people might get our number—I wrote a check at Pizza Hut, both our names are on it, teenage girls work there. Why did I write that dumb check? I also wrote one at a local convenience store. I wonder if the mail carrier has daughters? Does he go home at night and tell stories about the wild mail he delivers to the weaving school, *Vegetarian Times* and French postcards featuring naked women?

I am still angry at my ex-lover who has spent the last few weeks in Paris sending me graphic postcards that detail her forays into the lesbian club scene. I can't help feeling she has done this as an act of revenge. Or maybe she has just lived in California too long and has lost touch with what it means to have an address with a rural route number. She's from Oklahoma, she knows what she's doing. Then I think about how this little act of revenge, probably something she finds humorous, could actually be deadly. We're not trying to fool anyone here, not pretending. But our presence on this one hundred and eighty acres is only barely tolerated already because we are outsiders. What will happen now that they know we are lesbians?

Of course I have considered this question all along, have continued to hope that somehow we will make a place for ourselves. There have been no more calls, but the fear is always present. I cannot ignore my knowledge of violence against queers. I often think about Brandon Teena, the transgendered woman raped and killed in her small Nebraska farming community because she dated the town's young women. I have read about and witnessed the reactions of other rural communities to the presence of lesbians. I wonder if people here will see us as a threat.

The farmer who lives to the south of our house has become a friend. He lives alone, raises sheep, and tends a huge garden. He is a slow, easygoing Californian who moved here in the '70s after studying peasant agriculture in Central America and teaching at Berkeley. He is not the typical county resident, but he has managed to make a place for himself here and is friends with everyone. I felt sure that he would be an ally the first time we walked into his old farmhouse, the woodstove stoked on a cold Spring day and books and artwork piled up around the room. He wears tie-dye, swims naked in his pond, and gives good gardening advice.

We bonded over seeds and seed catalogs, and when his tomato seedlings came up in the spring he called to let me know that I could take some, along with his precious composted sheep manure. He calls to tell me that the tomato horn worm has arrived on his vines, and to look out for squash beetles after I water. We spent a night on the porch drinking beer and talking early in the summer. I told him Jill and I were lovers, and he said he assumed that was the case. He says its nobody's business, what we do. Says he wouldn't ask the other neighbors about their sex lives. I know he's being nice and resist the urge to remind him our lives are about much more than sex.

We buy our peaches at the farmer's market on the square; buy our gas at the Time Out Cafe and Gas Station where locals have their $2.99 coffee and eggs every weekday morning; and buy our bread from the man who bakes granola and foccacia in his homemade brick ovens. A local merchant told me he was the last milkman with a delivery route in Missouri, and was closed down by the state for not pasteurizing his milk. Now he and his family bake bread and pastries and deliver them locally.

It is important for me to know the people I live with, to be connected to them as well as the land. I don't want to be just another commuter passing through town on weekday mornings. I have heard many lesbians say that the lesbian community is their family, provides their sense of home. But that is not enough for me. I cannot ignore the faces of the farmers on the side of the road selling melon from their truckbeds, or the teenagers sauntering slowly across the square on a Saturday night. I do need lesbian friends and queer family. But to be truly at home in a community, I need to know the people living around me and I want them to know me. It is a delicate balance. I also want to protect myself and my privacy.

The nearest town is charged with racial tension. Earlier in the summer a minor noise disturbance in the projects elicited response from dozens of police officers and highway patrol armed with mace and handcuffs. In the aftermath, the ACLU, FBI, local activists, and preachers descended on the town in a flurry of hearings and investigations. The atmosphere is reminiscent of the south during the '60s. At a regional library board meeting, the superintendent of schools stood up and announced that the problem of access to gay and lesbian internet sites through school terminals was not an issue because "there are no gay people" in the town. Meanwhile, the president of the library board, a gay man who teaches as a small private college here, presided over the meeting in silence. This is a place of deep contradictions.

For my birthday in July, Jill bought me a small yellow inflatable raft with two plastic oars. It is my first boat. After cake, candles, and balloons with the cats and dogs, we took the raft out on our pond under the moonlight. We squished our toes into the soft mud as we climbed in, splashing green water on each other and screaming as we lurched into the craft. While we drifted there under the willow trees we listened to the sounds of wild night—bard owls, bullfrogs, coyotes. I thought about how this little prairie is watching us, waiting to see if we will call her home, waiting to see if we will try to claim this land from all the creatures who live here with us, or if we will learn to share it with them. I hope the same for us, that the people who live here will choose to share the land with us, to respect us, to honor our choices. For now, I cannot leave. The poet was right, this place is mapped inside me, an intersection of heart and topography. And even though there are still days I long for the freedom and spark of queer culture in a coastal city, I am finding my center here in this pasture, in the cool dark mud at the bottom of the pond, in the night sky, in the black soil under my tomatoes, on my own front porch. Finally, I am finding home.

L.K. BARNETT

~e~

Callaloo

Julia, my lover, keeps secrets from me and she talks in her sleep. She recites childhood songs and whispers common Trinadadian phrases. I watch her and wish I knew her thirty years ago as a child. When morning comes I ask Julia to share her dreams with me but she hordes them as if they were her secret treasures.

Julia, my lover, goes through more phases than the moon. Attributing her moodiness to the fact that she was born under the sign of Cancer offers me some solace but not nearly enough. I am growing nervous because Thanksgiving is approaching which means Julia will enter her darkest phases.

Julia, my lover, misses her family. And although I know she loves me she does not feel a sense of home with me. I woke up this morning praying that tomorrow will not be like the last three Thanksgivings.

Every Thanksgiving Eve Julia and I have a huge blow-out which results in me eating dinner the following day with the half of our friends who take pity on me, while Julia stays at home alone talking on the phone with the other half of our friends.

In couples' counseling we have begun to touch on issues surrounding Julia's fears of intimacy and my fears of abandonment. Julia recently admitted that Thanksgiving evokes feelings of nostalgia for her family and home. When I think about her past I understand why the holidays are so difficult for her and I wish I could fill the void her family has given her.

Julia, when revealing her lesbianism, was asked to leave her father's house the summer before she went off to college. She went away at the end of the summer as planned and decided, after some time had passed, that she'd write her family a letter. She wrote over thirty letters her first semester. They were all returned. She tried addressing them to different members of the family—her mother, her father, her younger sisters Bridget and Eliza and even her baby brother Joshua—with the hope that somebody would read the letter and answer her. Still the letters were returned to her unopened. Julia tried calling and as soon as her voice was deciphered she would hear a dial tone. The loudness of the dial tone seemed to magnify each time she called. The last time she called the tone was deafening. She decided she would make no more attempts. That was twenty years ago.

Julia has not recovered from the cruelty of rejection imposed on her by her family. While I feel for her I am selfish and I know I can not bear another fight this holiday. I need connectedness with her.

I watch Julia as she pulls herself out of the bed. We are both schoolteachers and today there is no school. She walks over to the window and pulls the string that opens the blinds. The sky is a light gray and it looks quite still outside; a typical New England winter morning. I want to go to the market and buy ingredients for tomorrow's feast. I take a deep breath before speaking.

"Julia, will you come to the market with me?"

"We don't need anything from the market." She snaps back.

"Of course we do baby. Tomorrow is Thanksgiving."

"Well, I'm not really into turkey Linda. You know that."

I take another deep breath and try a different approach.

"What dishes did you eat at home on holidays? I mean, I know you didn't celebrate Thanksgiving in Trinidad but what would you typically eat on a holiday?"

Julia scrunches her lips and nose together and gives me her "I'm thinking" pout. She comes back to the bed and collapses on it. Pulling the magenta down comforter over her head she softly says, "I miss callaloo." I am stunned but I reach under the comforter to take her in my arms. I ask, "What is callaloo?"

"Callaloo develops from a West African idea of stewing greens down to a smooth puree."

Having been raised by my grandmother, a southern woman who loved vegetables, I am familiar with all types of greens—mustards, collards, and turnips. I smile remembering how I loved my grandmother's greens. I miss her greens too and my smile lingers as I realize Julia and I have this in common.

"Callaloo is the leaf of a taro plant," Julia explains. Silence begins to fill our bedroom and I know she is recalling memories of home. In an effort to break the silence and bring her back to our home I make a suggestion.

"Let's make callaloo."

"I don't have a recipe. I never learned how to make it. All the women in my family learn to make it when they reach adulthood. I left home at seventeen—not yet an adult by my mama's standards."

"We'll find a recipe." My tone of voice is promising.

Julia begins to cry. Then she sobs. Soon her nose is red and her chest is heaving. This has been a long, long time coming. I hold her closer to me and encourage this release. *Callaloo* means home to her, I tell myself. And if they won't accept her I will do everything to evoke the feeling of home right here. I make that promise to the gods.

~☙~

After she is empty of tears and assured of my love for her, Julia and I get dressed and as we are doing so we bombard each other with vivid stories from our past family lives. We laugh, we cackle, and we hoot for the especially funny stories. We express condolences when stories of deceased childhood pets and lost friends are shared. Most importantly, we connect.

We drive to the nearest women's bookstore and begin our search for a callaloo recipe. We pull twenty cookbooks from the shelves and sit on the floor. When she's looked through four or five cookbooks Julia gives up. I know this by the way she throws both arms up in the air and then lets her hands collapse on her legs, causing a slapping sound. Just as she is about to say what I guess will be an "oh well," I turn a page and see:

Callaloo

serves four

1 pound fresh callaloo greens (Spinach may be substituted)

1 pound okra, topped & tailed

1 medium sized onion coarsely chopped

1 bouquet garni, prepared from scallions, fresh thyme, parsley
    and chives

Salt & pepper to taste

1 clove garlic, minced

1/2 pound cooked ham, cut into 1/4 inch dice-sized portions

Juice of 3 limes

6 1/2 cups of water

I begin to read the recipe aloud and Julia crawls over to where I am sitting and begins to squeal in delight. We buy the cookbook and head for the market.

~e~

After Thanksgiving dinner, which included callaloo, cornbread, and other food favorites that leap from our childhood memories, Julia and I make love. I have not filled Julia's void but I believe we are both beginning to heal, and for me home is the only place where healing can occur. While Julia sleeps I realize the importance of my home with her. Somehow our home and the love we've built has sustained me throughout all the difficult times. I close my eyes and hope to dream of callaloo and many more Thanksgivings with Julia.

VICKI REITENAUER

～

Home Movies

My first lover and I are lying like one extended body—her feet to sofa's end, her back-of-head to my crotch, my head to sofa's other end—on the nubby brown couch in my parents' basement. It is older than I am. I could have been conceived on it. There's a hole from a cigarette burn on the left arm; my pinkie fits it perfectly. My hands are trying to decide whether to accidentally brush her nipples or not. I have taken a head rub southward, but not suddenly: over the course of many headaches, over the course of many weeks. My head has never hurt so much, and she hadn't had a headache a day in her life until she met me. We are standing the headache/sex axiom on its head. We have no idea what we are doing.

The title of this movie is *When the World Breaks Apart*.

～

I am standing in a place which could be anywhere. I am smelling hot and used oil, all the sorts of things that drip from cars. I am smelling disused items, misplaced items, anything my grandmother doesn't want up in the house anymore. I am smelling the intercourse of all of these items. Smelling their persistent devolution. I am smelling his cigar, even after. I am saying to myself *I'm really here, I'm really here.*

The title of this movie is *The Smell of Fear.*

~ℓ~

I am standing by my car with which I hit another car; my junker, which clipped the New York Mercedes, which ran the stop sign into my right-of-way. I am taking my first lover to her night class at the college in the summer, the science requirement, three weeks and you're done. We are running late because her parents left the house for a few minutes and a few minutes have come to be all that we need. No one is hurt. The police come. Someone comes who takes her away, to her class at the college. I drive my car away leaking, go to my parents' house, close the drapes. The phone is ringing and stays ringing. I know it's my lover calling to make sure I am OK. The phone stops ringing and starts ringing again. When it stops minutes later I take it off the hook. I know she wants to talk to me. I know she's missing her class. I sit on my parents' upstairs sofa and listen to the phone not ring.

The title of this movie is *You Can't Find Me.*

∽

My sister and I are waiting for my grandparents. My mother's been asked to work her day off; someone called in sick at the bank. I think it's tremendously exciting that my mother touches money all day long, counts it, smells it. We are waiting for my grandparents to come because we are too young to stay alone. They are going to take us to get peaches. My sister is waiting for my grandparents to come. I am hiding somewhere. I am so well hidden even I don't know where I am. My grandparents arrive and gather my sister and look for me. I cannot hear them looking. They look and look and then they leave. My grandparents take my sister, go for peaches.

The title of this movie is *Keep Away from Grandpop.*

∽

My first lover is keeping herself from crying. We are sitting in a car on the edge of the campus of the college we both attend. Her brother, a cop, has asked her parents if they think something fishy is going on between her and me and they have asked her and she has said no. My lover is keeping herself from crying, it is what she has come to do best.

The title of this movie is *Something Fishy Is Going On.*

∽

We are eating a Saturday supper of Spam and baked beans and raw fried potatoes that my father puts mustard on. We are watching the

221 | Vicki Reitenauer

news on TV and the newscaster reads a story about Harvard or Yale. I say, full of nitrite bravado, that that's where I'm planning on going. My parents laugh, say I can't go there, it's only men who go there. My parents tell their friends and my relatives this story, laughing, implying my inability to stay away from the boys. Not implying that they wouldn't know that Harvard and Yale recently went coed because no one in my family's gone to college, no one's needed to know that kind of thing. Also not implying that I have at best a local-college confidence, because I'm still years away from that test.

The title of this movie is *Laughing When You Don't Get the Joke.*

~

My first lover and I are moving things along in my bedroom in my parents' house. My parents have gone to a viewing. I love whoever's died not for who they were but for their timing. My lover is raising my bra up the flagpole of my neck, she has no fingers for clasps. My lover is teaching me why women were given mouths. The front door is opening, is shutting. My clothes are coming on faster than they came off, like a funny video made funnier in reverse. I am greeting my parents halfway down the hall wearing my necklace of solid cotton comfort.

The title of this movie is *If You Didn't Laugh, You'd Cry.*

~

I am getting a cast put on my arm. The doctor tells me that it won't hurt a bit and then he wrenches the arm which hurts so much I don't notice its corrected slant. It hurts so much I don't feel a thing. He was right. I bet he went to Harvard or Yale. I am planning how I will get my sister back for breaking my arm by jumping off her Hoppity Horse onto me after I fell off mine after my grandmother told us not to jump on the Hoppity Horses with our feet but to hop on them like we're supposed to. I am planning how I will explain this. I am not thinking about my grandfather at all.

The title of this movie is *This Won't Hurt a Bit*.

~&~

My sister is coming home with her boyfriend. They're sleeping in separate rooms. When my first lover stays over because we're working on an assignment late or we're going somewhere early or she's forgotten the way to her own parents' house several miles away, she sleeps with me. We know how to do it quietly. We may only know how to do it quietly. My sister and her boyfriend go to a motel for a while and then come back to sleep apart.

The title of this movie is *It Pays to Be Invisible*.

~&~

My sister is two and I am four and we have a screen door that slams shut. My sister is behind me and I don't know it, or my sister is behind me and I do know it but I don't care. I slam the screen door shut and with it my sister's finger, the pinkie, hanging from a thread. Blood does spurt. My sister is screaming and my mother is wrapping her hand in a towel and my father is starting the car. I go along to the hospital or I don't. There isn't time to drop me off with my grandparents. I have nowhere else to be.

The title of this movie is *I Didn't Mean To.*

～

I am sitting on my parents' upstairs sofa between my mother and my father. I am sobbing and waiting to die soon from the pain of being left by my first lover for a woman who is married to a man. I am explaining to my parents about my sudden deconstruction. I am coming out. They are both sitting very close to me. My mother's looking stricken. My father's using his lowest voice, he's singing to me the number one song on the countdown: *Don't worry, be happy*.

The title of this movie is *Where the Strangest Things Happen.*

～

My second lover and I are in the living room of the apartment we share in a city neither of us belongs to. I am in the corner of the sofa her cat has clawed into shreds. Her cat is dead. Five months and I still look for fresh damage. My lover brought the sofa with her from a previous life. She paid a lot of money for it. My lover is coming towards me in slow motion but quickly, too. My lover is windmilling her arms like a rockstar or an exasperated cartoon character. My lover is telling me how much I want her to hit me, how it is all I really want, how it is all that will make me happy.

The title of this movie is *Sleeping in the Second Bedroom*.

∼ℓ∼

I am visiting my parents in the house I mostly grew up in. It is in the suburbs, but an old enough one that there are trees older than I am. I enter the house, kiss my mother hello, kiss my father hello. I walk to the kitchen and open the cubbyhole they had built in when they re-did the room last spring. I'm looking for something to eat: salty, sweet, doesn't matter. I have no idea when I ate last or whether I am hungry. I have no idea what the word *hungry* means. I need to get something in my mouth, I need to get it swallowed. I can make a meal out of these potato chips, I can make an exception to vegetarianism for the lard that they're cooked in.

The title of this movie is *You Are What You Eat*.

∼ℓ∼

My second lover and I are in my cold-in-winter hot-in-summer studio apartment. It's August and it's broiling. We are sitting inside the path the air's taking off the fan. We are laughing and sweating and doing something which makes us even hotter—the laundry, or fucking. And then eating Doritos at first for a snack and then, what the hell, for dinner. It's too hot to cook. It's good we fucked earlier because now we're too sick to, too full of bellyache to do anything but moan. I am so happy to be with her here in this heat, to be moaning.

The title of this movie is *You Are What You Eat, The Sequel.*

❧

My sister and I are celebrating New Year's Eve in my studio apartment. It's cold because I can't pay the heat; it's electric, I keep the thermostat way down. I convince her it's an adventure, New Year's Eve, pretend we're in Times Square. It's also my life. We have the TV turned on and the windows are high in the walls and the lights are off but a streetlamp shines in. We are bundled and bundled and I wish I could tell her what it feels like to live in my body, what sort of magic happens here. We are so cold that we shiver ourselves unconscious before the ball drops.

The title of this movie is *Not Minding the Cold.*

❧

I am coming to the apartment I live in with my second lover in a city neither of us belongs to. I am returning from a conference I had to attend for the job she hates my having. My second lover is waiting rigid on the bed when I walk in. She has escaped into rigidity. She is too rigid to cry. I am sitting down on the bed. She is telling me that she has read the journal I forgot to take with me. She is telling me she has read the journal I have left behind. I told it things I never told her. I told it things I told her but inside a very different light. She is crying and I am crying. She is melting. We partially make love. We have not made love for months in whole or in part. We are going to look for separate apartments when we finish almost making love.

The title of this movie is *I Meant It*.

~e~

I am at an extended-family picnic, my mother's side, the peasant part of my makeup. I am asking and asking what I never remember: who belongs to whom, whose sister this is, the birth order of the sixteen children in my grandmother's family and how they've descended into those who are here. Among them are the lesbians. My mother's cousin and my mother's other cousin, for sure, and who knows who else. I have my own suspicions. They are there like everybody else, loved and not loved. In families like ours you are connected by things much more important than love: you are connected by what you have survived and, having survived, how well you tell the story. We keep everybody who wants to be kept but whisper behind their backs just the same.

The title of this movie is *My Cousin, Myself*.

~e~

My third lover and I are in her apartment because it is bigger than mine. Also because she has two cats and I have none. My lover is sure that her cats love me best. I am trying to win the cats' affection. I have given up on trying to make dinner because my lover is the more graceful cook. While we eat she touches me with her bare foot, presses it into me, but like it's an accident, like I'm an apparition of a woman who used to visit her lover here a century ago. I want to take my lover's foot and stick it inside me, enter her into my body backwards. When we go to bed my lover doesn't feel my tenderness, falls asleep with the news.

The title of this movie is *Now You See Her, Now You Don't*.

~~

I am sitting within a circle of women who all have pens moving on paper. It's a writers' group, a space carved out of a month where words crack open like pumpkin seeds between our teeth and we chew the meat out. The women are queer and not-queer in every conceivable way. It is the most difficult place I have ever lived. We take our show on the road, read our work like a symphony in front of people we know and don't know. At the chain bookstore we have a mike which feeds us through the store and people come to stand on the fringes of the triangular clearing filled with seats between Sports and True Crime and Romance. Some listen, some leave, and some say they never knew this kind of thing existed.

The title of this movie is *Where You Least Expect It*.

~~

I am leaving my third lover in my apartment in a city I don't belong to early in the morning to go to another city with my sister for the day and night. To go to New York to see a show and to hang out like we used to. My lover has gifted my body with a trail of bruises during a long night of sex with teeth. They are the first hickies I have ever received. I am driving to the bus station to meet my sister and planning how to explain it and feeling quite well-fucked when I realize that my lover has sucked my skin raw because she doesn't believe that I am going to spend the weekend with my sister. My lover believes that I have lied to her and have a woman in every port. My lover believes this because she has a woman in every port and has just told or will soon tell me a version of the lie she suspects me of telling.

The title of this movie is *Taking the Early Bus Out.*

∾

My father has been diagnosed with cancer in his throat. I am at my parents' house helping out. I am thinking how this is what we do, these people that I am from. I am thinking how this is what we do even when we are lesbians and we lie and we move away from the site of our lying. I am thinking about what starts a cancer growing: nitrites, tobacco, secrets, cheap beer, bad blood, genes. I am stopping myself from continuing the list because it's just too fucking depressing. I am staying in the room I lost my virginity in, I am on my hands and knees trying to find it. The walls are repapered and there's a carpet on the floor where there was none. My virginity has been remodeled. But I do find her who licked it from me peering down from the ceiling. Even if I have never been a virgin. Even if memory doesn't have that long a history.

The title of this movie is *The House of Mirrors*.

～&～

I am leaving my third lover. I am leaving my third lover in the momentarily-unoccupied office of the boss that we share. She is out to lunch. I am leaving my lover because she lives in a world where there is no such thing as what's true. I am leaving my lover because I will cease to exist if I don't. I am leaving my lover stone-faced and sucker-punched. I don't care who gets the last word. I am leaving my lover in our busy not-for-profit workplace. I am taking my tenderness elsewhere.

The title of this movie is *Leaving Her Behind*.

～&～

I want to say something beyond these broken bones of stories. I want to say: Home is memory lounging in its unkept house. Home is the house you first cried in and it is the everything surrounding the negative space when that house has been happily burned down. Home is the food your body craves even after you've decided that it's bad for you, even after you've american dreamed yourself into affording something different, the comfort it brought you then, brings you now. Home is needing that comfort. Home is the flesh and the shadow of every woman you've loved or will love. Home is the bell-ringing moment of anything true moving through the lesbian body. Home is the body which situates itself in a place of what-can-happen when women gather themselves together in a bed, in a house, on paper.

Home is where you keep your stuff.

～～

I am an off-season rental living in the second house from the beach on an island deserted for winter. I am alone on the street except for the man in the apartment upstairs, the owner of the house who is dying, slowly, but who isn't dead yet. I am here to forget about lovers. I am here to turn my lovers into poems. The apartment is full of his shipwrecked furniture; I pay a man in a town near the city I never belonged to forty dollars a month to lock my few belongings up tight. If I were given five minutes to look this place over, study everything, memorize the contents of the room and then were led away and asked to tell a stranger what was in here, I couldn't do it. Except that there is a clock on the wall of the kitchenette and its batteries wound down weeks ago. I live at three o'clock. I get up when I want to, write, walk on the beach, eat when I'm hungry, write, get plenty of fluids, stay in various stages of undress, write. I am also not dead yet.

Home Is Where You Are Still Alive.

tatiana de la tierra

~&~

The Home That Is a Shadow in My Soul

Mountains, green with wild sugar cane, red with ripe coffee beans and copper, black and bronze with layers of rich earth, are my beginning. In the mountains, gusts of wind purify and the moist emerald ground nourishes intravenously. Waters, always clear, cool, and in motion, transform the cosmic nectar that blesses the country where I emerged.

My story begins in El Tolima, a region in the heart of Colombia embroidered with the central range of the Andean mountains. In 1863 my great-great grandparents came to Villahermosa, a tiny town tucked so high in the fertile mountains that the heavens became confused. They were founders of this place known as the town of two lies because, as the saying goes, it was neither *villa* nor *hermosa*.

Magical mountainous earth, that black dirt endowed with ancient volcanic ash, was the soil by which my ancestors lived. My great grandparents, Mamá Rosita and Papá Gabino, owned coffee plantations and lived on their farm near Villahermosa. Ripe red, the coffee beans were hulled with a hand-cranked machine and left to dry for days in the sun until becoming pale brown, when they'd be placed in burlap sacks and sent into nearby towns on the backs of mules to be sold. Also growing on that virgin wombed earth were plantain trees that shaded the coffee, yellow corn that transformed into *arepas* daily, rooted yuca for the weekly *sancochos*, and sugar cane that became hardened golden brown *panela* on the monthly *moliendas*.

Amidst all of that earth tilling and cow tending, Mamá Rosita birthed Genoveva, Teñito, Belia, Benjamín, and Elvia, who would be my grandmother. In 1925, when the children were school age, the family moved to El Libano, a nearby town that had good schools, healthy commerce, and an even bigger church. They traveled to El Libano on horseback, taking a descending path that tinkled with the sounds of streams, rivers, and sparkling waterfalls. Founded in 1855, El Libano nestles cozily in a valley that's embraced by mountains and neighbored by rushing rivers, wide-mouthed craters, and ice-tipped volcanic peaks. It was a bustling town, seven days on foot and three days on horseback away from any major Colombian city.

An emerald-green wooden door marks the entrance to my great grandparents' home. This house, where I took my first steps, coddled the generations before me. The children who ended up being my elders lived in that house in El Libano with a farm in the backyard that bore scallions, carrots, green beans, tomatoes, peas, and chayotes. Guayabas, oranges and apple bananas grew on trees that reached to the blue sky and then dropped their fruit on the ground in that infinite backyard. Chickens laid eggs nightly as white as Margaritas, and colorful Dahlias grew tall and abundantly. Every evening a herd of baby calves walked down the long hall into the patio, where they awaited their mothers, who arrived at six a.m. the next morning to be milked. Those moos, along with a choir of crowing roosters, inaugurated each day.

When I was seven years old, in 1968, I moved with my family to the United States. From there on, Colombia became a shadow that looms in my soul. I visit in the summers during my teenage years and then in between semesters during my undergraduate years. And then, after coming out, I wait a few years for my next visit. I hesitate, worry about the relatives. And then I go with a gringa girlfriend and really, it's cool. We have sex on my great-great grandmother's bed and it's so perverse and fine. I tell her that's as deep as I can ever be fucked and that's the truth. A huge framed color portrait of Jesus' bleeding heart looks on. Everyone seems to know something is up but no one questions me about it, and for the first time ever, I don't make any announcements. Years later, my relatives still ask about my now long-gone girlfriend. And I learn to bring my dyke self with me wherever I go, even to the sacred soil that brings me in contact with the artifacts of my history.

Later, in my thirties, I make an emergency trip to El Libano. Teñito, my great aunt, is gravely ill. I fly into Bogotá and take a taxi to the bus station, where I look for the fastest ride into town. The "Expresso Tolima" buses that I remember used to be big and clunky, with wide, sagging seats that creaked during the entire seven-hour ride. Fine dust, blown in by the wind, would swirl through my hair. The drivers were usually middle-aged men who had icons of the virgin Mary on the dashboard and played *bambucos* and *boleros* all the way. This time, I ride in a shiny white Ford minivan that seats no more than thirteen passengers. It is air conditioned, there are seat belts, and there is no saint on the dashboard for our protection. The driver is in his twenties and the music is harsh. Rock, disco, techno, merengue. He passes out plastic bags for motion sickness and rushes off, assuring us he can get us there in four hours by taking a new route.

On the way, I watch the landscape from the front seat. After we get out of Bogotá, the road begins to wind through the mountains. But the scenery is not as green as I remember it; the slopes are patched with pale mustard and browned grasses. And it's hotter than it ever used to be. It's still beautiful, though, and I doze off during the ride, praying for my great aunt and wondering how El Libano will look to me now that it's 1996.

I wake up hours later, just as we are passing through what used to be Armero, a small pueblo that was buried alive when el Volcan del Ruiz erupted ten years ago. Now, it is an impromptu cemetery, with thousands of white wooden crosses dotting the area overgrown with tall grasses and weeds. We are fifteen kilometers from El Libano, and from here on it is a winding uphill drive. Scenes begin to look familiar to me. The wooden house with the pink veranda and white rose bushes. A young barefoot boy leading a mule loaded with burlap sacks. Blackberry bushes jutting from the mountain. Fields of miniature coffee trees. Groves of guayabas.

A white sign reads, *El Libano, Tolima. Founded in 1855. Population 34,813. Welcome.* At the entrance of the town is the cemetery, where all of my ancestors are buried. We pass the new Hotel Los Fundadores, the hospital, a park and then, my favorite bakery, "Mis Golosinas." Then we turn on la Calle Real and I see people lined up outside of Telecom, a red building where long-distance calls are made. We pass the pharmacy on the corner, the little stationery store next to it, then the butcher shop, a music store that's blaring Shakira's "Estoy Aquí." Finally, the driver parks the minivan in the main plaza and I get out with my hand luggage. I am home, the home that is a shadow in my soul.

It's 1996, but as far as I'm concerned, it's 1965 and I am a little girl living in this little town tucked in the mountains. It's late Friday afternoon and the plaza is bustling. Vendors bake *arepas* over charcoal grills, smother them with butter, and charge 400 pesos a piece. Potatoes and green plantains are sliced and deep fried, then sprinkled with salt and served in miniature brown paper bags for 300 pesos. It is all the food of my childhood—crispy round corn *buñuelos*, grilled corn on the cob, half-moon *empanadas*, blood sausages, stuffed yuca, caramelized roasted peanuts, sweet coconut *cocadas*, cold milky *avena*. I buy a little bit of everything and bite one thing after the other, marveling at the time that seems to stand still here.

In the plaza the townspeople are out for an afternoon stroll. Children play along on the grass. Old ladies sit on benches and gossip. Couples hold hands. Teenagers gather in a corner, wearing the latest hip clothes. Young men court their wives-to-be. Men talk amongst themselves. There are no strangers here. There are also no dykes that I know of, no rainbow flags flapping anywhere, and frankly, I don't care. This is about going home, about meeting with matriarchs. It's not about rhetoric or politics or domestic partnerships. It's about growing up and sustenance. It's about the first steps that I ever took. It's about embroidering orange flowers on starched white placemats. It's about fat and frayed black-and-white photo albums. It's about playing among the burlap sacks full of coffee beans, getting lost in coffee fields, drinking *café con leche* out of a baby bottle.

Before walking to my great aunt's house, I head into the church that occupies a full side of the square. It is the tallest building in the entire town, with two steeples, painted with peach walls and a copper trim. Inside, light filters through stained glass windows. I light a candle and kneel before la Virgen del Carmen, my great aunt's favorite saint. On the walk to her house I notice that everything looks the same as I remember it. I wave at the saleswomen at the fabric store on the corner and think about all the skirts and dresses I've had made in this town. I pass *la galeria*, where fruit, vegetables, grains, herbs, legumes, meat, and household odds and ends are sold. Finally, I pass a small coffee warehouse and then I am in front of the emerald-green wooden door, number 1352, behind which lies all of my family history.

As I walk in I sense a stillness, and when my cousin greets me dressed in black I know that my great aunt has passed on. She had died just as I was landing in Bogotá earlier that day. By now, she is already in a cedar coffin, wearing a deep green dress with a pattern of tiny yellow flowers. She is in the front room, the official sitting room that was always kept locked except for special occasions. Red candles are lit around the coffin, and many of my relatives are already there, dressed in black and praying the rosary. Teñito, eighty-five years old, rests inside her special room, and I kneel before her and tell her so many things that, in life, never needed to be said. She was the thread that kept all of our history alive, the only remaining matriarch of her generation. She knew all the stories that made up our family history. She had lived through *la violencia,* Colombia's civil war, through dozens of presidents and political upheavals. She was alive before electricity and telephones existed. She never knew E-mail or faxes. She never knew that I was a lesbian. And she lived her entire life in El Libano, this place so far removed.

All through the night, relatives come from different parts of Colombia, filling the little room with prayers. Teñito will be buried the following day; all the arrangements have already been made. By noon on Saturday, four of my uncles and male cousins are carrying the coffin down the street. A priest leads the procession of family and friends. We stop at the church for a service in my great aunt's honor, and then we all continue on foot, to the cemetery. I think of all the funerals that I went to with Teñito, and the weekend visits that we made to the cemetery. We carried flowers fresh from the backyard and brought them to the family mausoleum. She prayed as she changed the water and disposed of the old flowers. I had never learned the prayers but I knew the ritual well. When I was a little girl, coming to the cemetery was an outing and I played upon the graves and memorized my great-great grandparent's names. This visit is different. It symbolizes the end of an era.

On this Saturday afternoon, beneath blue skies and amidst eternal prayers, my great aunt is buried in El Libano. Her mother's remains are placed at her feet so that she will be accompanied into the other world as she was in this one. I cry, not only for her passing and for everything that she means to me, but for the shift my soul must make as I face the rest of my life without a living symbol of my past. Walking back towards Teñito's house I see El Libano in its age-less beauty—the wooden houses, the horses clicking on the street, the life that I have always known and that will always remain the same. And once again, I thank God for blessing me with such a birthplace.

LAUREN CRUX

∽

The Swimming Lesson

"In order to love me, she must relinquish, or at the very least examine the presumed privilege that accompanies her skin and class. In order to love her, and myself, I must resist the temptation to make it easy for her."

—P. ROSS

I am in love with an African-American woman who does not swim. Imagine that; I, Madame Poisson, water-baby, have a lover who does not swim, who does not want to learn, who is afraid of the water. When I offer to teach her she tells me she sinks like a rock.

First Lesson

In the shallow waters of Hawaii, to my amazement she does indeed sink like a rock. Later she tells all our friends that while on vacation the first thing I did was try to drown her.

Second Lesson

In a warm pool in Arizona I encourage her: "Try again, but this time fill up your lungs with air then you will not sink." She inhales deeply and stays afloat. This time she is amazed. I continue; "Let the water be your friend, let it embrace you, buoy you up." But she is rigid, frightened. She says, "You know the history of my people, we don't swim. And our hair, we don't like to get it wet because that ruins it." But her hair is now cut close and as she dips into the water it is not ruined. She says, "I am afraid, I don't want white people to watch you teaching me." We wait until we are alone.

Third Lesson

I promise not to let her go, hold her while she kicks her feet. With practice she begins to relax. I grasp her hands as she kicks and swims into my arms. There I hold her. She tenses. I remind her, "We are in shallow water, any time you want, drop your feet and stand." She experiments; puts her feet down, says, "Oh," with gentle humor.

Swim Test

"OK, I know that to ask you to learn to bodysurf is going too far, but water is my home. If I am blue or dispirited, I head to water—to the ocean, rivers, lakes, even a bathtub will do. It's where I lay my body down, a place I can fly without falling, and where I feel graceful and beautiful. I'd like to know you were safe when we hang out near water. And how about this, when we're in the ocean, you could ride on my back and we could laugh all the way to shore. But bottom line, you don't have to like water to love me, I just want you to be with me."

This makes a difference to her. Learning to swim to be with me, this she will consider. I have invited her in. But she is not easy. Reminding me of her history she challenges, "Do you really hear what I am telling you? Do you understand? It is not just my family fear that I am carrying, that none of us could learn to swim, but something much older, much bigger."

I founder; I can feel the danger and I know the strangulations of race. I have some knowledge of her people's history, of her own anguish and outrage, yet what do I know beyond the texts, beyond the words?

When I ask, she tells me that as a child she never conceived of swimming as an activity, as fun. When we hike together and she watches me drop my clothes and jump into every swimming hole that comes along, she explains that she has never imagined swimming as freedom, certainly not as home. Centuries ago, she was stolen from her land and forcibly carried over water to a new and violent place. Water was death to her, not home.

We are both quiet. After a time I say gently, "Let's both be strong with the histories we carry. I am learning how to love you, to know and hold the wounds; I learn to face myself, naked and scarred. Let yourself learn to swim and heal your fear. Each of us teaching the other how to breathe."

Fourth Lesson

In the photo studio where I am doing her portrait for a publication she is to be in, we play. "OK," she jests, "Swimming Lesson." She lies belly down on one of the pedestals and begins to kick her feet and paddle her arms. With a mock grimace she takes a breath just as I click the shutter. We begin to laugh and she turns over, tries the backstroke, then over again for the breast stroke. The black and white photo from this session is hilarious and frightening.

We return later, both in our swim suits. My skin coral white, hers café au lait with a hint of red, our bathing suits to our surprise are an identical shade of metallic blue. We lie down on the pedestals, each facing a different way, the camera set on automatic. And we swim slowly, easily at first, then hard. Backstroke, Australian crawl. Gravity, the great leveler, leaves us both awkward, laughing. Where are these women swimming to? And why? And where can they go to really, on their pedestals, out of water? Is there a place for them they can both call home?

We stand, tall and short, facing the camera, front and front, back and front, back to back. We strive for all the permutations. But describe only a few.

I love her for this, love us for this; how she and I can take our enormous pain and turn it to waves of laughter, speak of that which has hurt us so deeply, and which also brings us together.

D. KILLIAN

∼e∼

This Is America

Back here in the land

neon and naive

I'm just a train car

passing through

too much changed

geography

in a single night

These American voices

screech on my steel

overplanted lives press past me

field after field

I need someone—remind me:

Honky—

this is home.

I am traveling across America by train. For months now, I have been readying for the journey; feeling in my body the pull of track and weight, the rhythmic patter, increasing speed and destination. Even longer, I have been planning this: a home-coming. But to what? A peace making, a reconciliation, between myself, the body, and the land. As if seeing the country whole, linked by a thousand miles of wood and steel, will tie the broken pieces.

I am America. This is it. But I do not know my hands or feet. But want to: stand up, with no medals or bands playing; stand up and say (with quiet, easy acceptance) that this is it: America. America!

∾

The night before (the night I left—the train departs at three a.m.), I pack my things. I carry a bag of clothes, another with books and cassettes; sandwiches, pound cake, and six-ounce bottles of fruit juice. It's a long trip.

Leaving Chicago, it's not quite dark but all the lights are on: the lights at the foot of the driveways, the lights outside the back doors. In the humming street lamps, I see the spare freezers of America—in the basements, in the garages out back—stacked full, ready, with two or three ice trays, pork chops, and Buds. Enough food for months, in case we need it. Enough food: beef jerky, canned peaches, and plums. The wagon trains, heading west. I too am raising dust. My wheels are turning. But I'm traveling alone, and I know it.

~&~

Across the aisle, there are two college kids, stretched out across seats reserved (the sign above informs us) for "couples." They're fine and young and white; with glossy-page clothes, straight teeth, Ohio State sweatshirts, and skis. It's winter break and they're in love, obviously. They merge beneath their thin, synthetic blanket, her head turned to the nape of his neck.

Down the middle of the aisle, an elderly couple—in their seventies? but at least retired—move towards the next door. Bobbing side to side, clutching (with free hands) each consecutive seat, they resist the train's motion and are not thrown. Yet still, despite the odds, they manage to (feebly) embrace; his arm resting along the back ledge of her waist.

People stare at me. But why? Because for two days, I've not bathed (like everyone else who got on in Chicago)? Because I'm a big, not-wearing-a-bra woman and beneath two shirts and a wool vest it shows: my difference, my defiance, my wanting to be seen? It's political. But I don't want it to be. All I want is my comfort and ease, three days and four nights on the train, without latex and elastic slicing my sides; the soft, curved friends (the breasts) not a detriment or regret. Or do they see my gem? The small, pink triangle on my black wool vest? Is it not one thing, but everything? My hair? The glasses? The clothes? I'm a woman traveling alone and they know it.

∼℮∼

I'm reading an anthology (published by the Quakers): *A Certain Terror: Heterosexism, Militarism, Violence, and Change.* Already my body knows the lines and pages, anger and frustration choking up. There's a poem on page thirty-five and I want (so badly) to read it: to stand up, to say, in the middle of the train, in the middle of the Midwest of America, to read it so loud (exhumed from my body like the Pledge of Allegiance for eighteen public school years, "…to the flag, of the United States of America, and to the nation, for which it stands…") A POEM, ladies and gentlemen! A POEM, by Pat Parker: "For the Straight Folks Who Don't Mind Gays But Wish They Weren't So Blatant."

Snap! Like fingers cracking! I have their attention. I'm standing on my seat (supporting myself with the overhead luggage rack and the head rest in front of me). Heads crane. Conversations cease. Even the elderly couple—at the door now to the next carriage— freeze. I pause at my pulpit and, then, begin:

> HAVE YOU met the woman
> who's shocked by two women kissing
> & in the same breath,
> tells you that SHE's pregnant?
> BUT GAYS SHOULDN'T BE BLATANT

Or this STRAIGHT COUPLE

sits next to you in a movie

& you can't hear the dialogue

'cause of the sound effects

BUT GAYS SHOULDN'T BE BLATANT

Or you go to an amusement park

& there's a tunnel of LOVE

& pictures of straights

painted on the front

and grinning couples

coming in and out

BUT...

...two very important train officials, one with a walkie-talkie, each in navy blue, are ebbing back from the top of the car. Even before they reach their target, I know the poetry is over.

On the train, of course, we're not allowed to use a walkman without a headset. But no one told me anything about reciting poetry. I tell the officials this, but it doesn't help. Already they're taking my bags, talking calmly to me like trained police. I'm a high tech instrument and they know it. Any second now, I'll detonate.

But I don't. I don't. I don't stand up. I don't shout out. I don't read. I stay in my place; I imagine. I dream. The fantasy evaporates— like a pool of water on a bursting hot road that, as you approach it, becomes bigger and bigger and then—at the moment of touching it—disappears.

～

I put down the book, pack it away in the plastic bag with the last of the sandwiches, the empty juice containers. I edge my way down-stairs, into the belly of the train, feeling my way to the rest room. I hadn't planned on this: how dirty and sweaty I'd feel; how desperate to be clean.

In the rest room there's a pocket-thin bar of Ivory soap and stacks of pale yellow Dixie cups. I strip from the waist up and begin to wash. In between little buckets and soap suds, a woman comes in. Uninvited, while fixing her hair at the sink, she tells me about her husband who had cancer, and how, after nine months of visiting him every day at the nursing place, he's finally died and she's going to live now with her son and daughter-in-law in California who have a trailer all ready for her, even the curtains, only twenty minutes away from the the beach and she's so happy to be moving now, now that her husband is dead, and—

"Are you going to California too, dear?" she suddenly stops.

I am, I tell her. To Oakland. San Francisco. Then Santa Cruz.

She smiles, limply.

"Oh, but *dear*, you don't want to go *there*, to Santa Cruz!"

I should know better, but I don't.

"Why? What do you mean?" I ask her. "I heard it's beautiful, with the university, on the sea…"

"Oh, it *is* beautiful. I mean, it *used* to be. But it's changed so, really. *Changed.*" She's shaking her head in disbelief, as if the whole city has dropped off the coast into the sea.

"My friends used to live there, but they had to move, it got so bad…"

I'm beginning to think this exodus could only have been an improvement, but I'm reading it: American Morse Code. Too big to bite into whole. Circling around, nibbling, like at a cocktail party hors d'oeuvre. I'm tempted to spell it out, to say it the way she means it: you mean blacks and Hispanics have moved in? Puerto Ricans? But I don't. I tap out the code.

"You mean there's *violence? Drugs? Gangs?* Like Los Angeles…? It's dangerous?"

"No, no, not like *that*," she tells me. "More like…*San Francisco*. Not *dangerous*. Just *odd*. *Funny*. The people there…" She looks at me, hopefully. Surely now I've got it. Surely now I know what she means.

I do. Better than she knows. I turn to face her squarely, water dripping down my front; little droplets swelling at my breasts. I

understand. Everything. But what does she know? Blind and ignorant. Would it help if I had a pink triangle tattooed on my biceps? A
piercing through my left nipple? Do I have to wear a T-shirt, a bill-
board across my forehead in florescent green, boldly stating DYKES
ARE US—everywhere, even on Amtrak, even in the rest room, in
the Midwest of America, rolling out, from Detroit, Cleveland,
Chicago, just after Denver? Naked. And invisible.

I pull on my clothes.

But before I leave, I see the pink triangle glimmering on my
wool vest. I pull it off and push it into my hip pocket, down deep.

∾

Back upstairs, I grab some provisions and head for the observation
deck. I'm hungry and need some space.

We're out of the Midwest now, into the desert, and never before
have I seen so much sand. Beach stretching everywhere. Ready to let
your sails out; to drown you. But no umbrellas, radios, or sand castles.
No boats on the horizon. Just undulating waves of damp sand. I
wonder: How does it manage it? The wet. Are there rivers beneath
the ground, beneath the bone dry skies and layers of waterless rock,
that rise up?

In this moving glass dome, there's plenty of room. I stretch out
on a double seat, my knees lazily apart, my toes against the window
frame.

To my right is a young mother with two boys, maybe six and eight. They're a picture portrait of a '50s family: the boys with neat crew cuts, striped T-shirts; the mother so well dressed and clean, a testimony, after four nights on the train, to American determination. The only difference is, unlike the '50s, this family is beautifully dark; if not for the vague east coast accents, the middle-class outfits, and the boxes of Kentucky Fried Chicken and Kool-Aid in hand, they could easily be from Nicaragua or Peru.

To my left is a neighbor who's not so friendly: a white man in a polyester blue suit who takes a hard second look at me. It's clear he's listening in as the two boys and myself call out the wild life that we see as the train speeds by.

"Look! A rabbit! Did you see it?"

"Over there! An eagle!"

The boys' mother tells me their story: how their father is in the army; how often they travel. About packing food. There's fresh water on the train so she brings powdered Kool-Aid, dry. Lighter to carry that way. They tire of sandwiches, so she brings chicken. The boys like it, traveling. They're used to it.

For some reason, they like me. Without speaking, the younger son offers me a cookie. Chocolate chip. Ummmmm. My favorite, I tell him; I'm the cookie monster! He laughs. Why don't I have purple hair then? He gives me another. I dye it, I tell him. He smiles, shakes his head. You're too OLD to watch Sesame Street! says the other one. It's for KIDS. Too old? Too old? How old do you think I am? He jumps up and down in his seat. His mother tells him to sit still.

We play private eye. Ten houses, two roads, and fifty million million million lamp posts but only five trees. How many coyotes do you think live in the desert? And those big hairy spiders?

We run out of questions. The older one wants his electronic game; his mother gets it for him. The younger one needs to go to the toilet. Will I watch the older one? Just five minutes? He's old enough to watch himself, but I'm here anyway. Sure. No problem. What can go wrong in five minutes?

～

Little aliens appear and disappear on the screen. The older boy is totally absorbed: rapidly jabbing buttons on the face of this little computer game. His body jerks in response. Bam! Bam! Bam! I move in closer to see. Who's attacking who? Are there creatures? Or just space vehicles?

But as if breaking some kind of radar, an unspoken taboo, just when I move to sit down beside him, he shouts out. "FAGGOT!" he shouts. "FAGGOT!!" he shouts again.

"Faggot! Faggot! FAGGOT!"

I jump back. Is he speaking to me? "FAGGOT! FAGGOT!" he repeats. "FAGGOT!" He doesn't look up. I look at him. Shock.

Disbelief. My body tingling and freezing. "FAGGOT!" Does he know this word ? "FAGGOT!" Does he know what it means? "FAGGOT!!" Where did he learn it? From his father? From the other kids on the base? On the street? Does he know what it means? Does he know that it's *me*? "FAGGOT!" The woman he offered his cookies? "FAGGOT!" The woman trusted by his mother? "FAGGOT!" "FAGGOT!" Faggot. Female. Faggot.

He's playing his game, and losing fast. FAGGOTS are the enemies. FAGGOTS are the ones who beat him; the ones he misses. "FAG-GOTS!" That's all. "FAGGOT!" Just a game. A sound. A name. Faggot! "FAGGOT!" the boy shouts again, his whole body responding, a rope pulled tight. "FAGGOT!" He jumps from his seat. "FAGGOT!" I wish to God he'd win. Stop. Shut up. I'm losing air in my throat, each shout, restricting; wet concrete seeping into my lungs. I wonder, again: does he know what it means? Queer aliens. Queer aliens invading—little homosexuals. Baby dykes. In the toilet. On the train. Amtrak. In the Midwest of America. In San Francisco. Santa Cruz. Chicago. Denver. Detroit. Gay aliens everywhere. Beside him on the seat. Little queers invading his little screen. His little towns? Where did he learn it? From his father? At school? At camp? From the other kids on the street?

I back away. I sit down. I notice: the man in the polyester suit looks satisfied. He knew *something* wasn't right. Unshaved legs spread comfortably wide. A woman taking her space. Female. Faggot.

I look down. I look away. But I don't want to. I want to get up. I want to tell the boy stories. I want to ask him, without trumpets or fanfare: Do you know that word, what it means? I want to tell him, gently, "This is America." I want to tell him, this word is not abstract. Not nameless. Not shit. Asshole. Jerk. Sucker. It's me: female. Faggot. "Faggot!" The pink triangle bites hard in my pocket; the little gem, a blade. I bite my lip. "Faggot!" Where is his mother? I want to leave. Escape. The Christian in the lion's den. The Jews in the cattle car. The wagon trains, surrounding. Miles and miles of desert and thousands of miles of wood and steel and nowhere to escape.

This is it: America.

~2~

L.K. Barnett is a graduate of women's history at Sarah Lawrence College. She has contributed to *The Harvard Gay and Lesbian Review*, *Lesbian Short Fiction* and *Does Your Mama Know: An Anthology of Black Lesbian Coming Out Stories*.

Elaine Beale is originally from England and has lived in the San Francisco Bay area for the last nine years. She is a writer, editor, fundraiser and the author of the mystery novel, *Murder in the Castro*.

All American Girl, **Robin Becker's** fourth collection of poems, won the 1996 Lambda Literary Award in Lesbian Poetry. She has received fellowships in poetry from the Massachusetts Artists Foundation, the National Endowment for the Arts, and the Bunting Institute of Radcliffe College. Becker has served on the Board of the Associated Writing Programs and currently serves as Poetry Editor for the *Women's Review of Books*. She is an Associate Professor of English at The Pennsylvania State University, where she teaches in the MFA Program.

At the sweet age of forty-eight, **Lauren Crux** left work, house, home, family, and friends, to run off to graduate school. Now she's fifty and has completed her MFA in studio arts from the University of California at Irvine. She's a writer, photographer, and performance artist, and is looking for work.

Monalesia Earle is a native New Yorker whose poetry has appeared in *Off Our Backs, Backbone, Plexus, The Optimist, Northview, New Horizons,* and *Spectrum*. Her fiction has appeared in *Close Calls: New Lesbian Fiction*. She is currently at work on her first novel.

Liz Galst is a frequent contributor to *Out* magazine. Her work has also appeared in *Ms, Mother Jones, The Village Voice,* and *The Boston Globe*, among others. She worked for two years as a staff writer at the *Boston Phoenix* and received a 1994 National Lesbian and Gay Journalists Associate Honors Award for her coverage of the religious right. She's currently a student in the Creative Writing Program at Columbia University.

M. Paz Galupo teaches psychology at Towson University. She lives in Baltimore, Maryland where she makes her home with her five-year-old daughter, Isabel.

Tzivia Gover is a freelance journalist living in western Massachusetts. She is a frequent contributor to *The Boston Globe, The Advocate* and *The Daily Hampshire Gazette*. Her poetry and prose have also appeared in anthologies including *Family: A Celebration* and *My Lover is a Woman*. She received her MFA in creative nonfiction from Columbia University.

Elizabeth Howell is a lesbian poet and artist who has a passion for gardens and compost. She works as a public librarian.

Mary Hussmann is the co-editor of *The Iowa Review* and an adjunct assistant professor at The University of Iowa. She has published poetry, essays, book reviews, and interviews in *Alaska Passages: 20 Voices from above the 54th Parallel, Echoes, The North American Review, The Iowa Review,* and *The Kenyon Review.*

D. Killian lived in Ireland six years and there received a Master of Philosophy degree in Anglo-Irish literature at Trinity College, Dublin. Her fiction and nonfiction has appeared in *Lesbian Short Fiction, Lambda Book Report, Sojourner* and *off our backs*. She is a contributing writer to the *Free Times*, Cleveland's alternative news and arts weekly.

Valerie Miner is a Western novelist and short story writer who teaches writing and literature at the University of Minnesota. Her novels include *Range of Light, A Walking Fire, All Good Women, Winter's Edge, Murder in the English Department, Blood Sisters* and *Movement*. She is also the author of *Tresspassing and Other Stories* and *Rumors From the Cauldron: Selected Essays, Reviews, and Reportage.*

Merril Mushroom is a writer living in Tennessee.

Judith Nichols was born in Boone County, Missouri, grew up in Granville, Ohio, and attended Earlham College and Pennsylvania State University. She is now an assistant professor of English at Vassar College. She recently completed a collection of poems, *The Love Circus.*

Katia Hope Noyes has been published in *Paramour, High Performance, Sex Spoken Here,* and *The SF Weekly*, where she was an arts columnist from 1993-1996. In 1995 and 1996 Noyes was a finalist for the Astraea Lesbian Writers Award. "As the Roots of the Trees" is an essay quickly becoming a novel, *Crashing America.*

Louise Rafkin is a journalist and author of several books including *Other People's Dirt.* She calls several places "home" including the Bay Area, Provincetown, and New York City.

Vicki Reitenauer has worked as a music teacher, advocate in the battered women's movement, abortion counselor/medical assistant and sexuality educator. She is a poet and a cofounding member of the women's writing and performance collective *It Ain't Pretty*, which appears in the Philadelphia area. Her poems have appeared in *Sojourner, Hurricane Alice, Earth's Daughters* and *Malachite and Agate.*

Linda Smukler is the author of two books of poetry: *Normal Sex* and *Home In Three Days. Don't Wash.*, a multimedia project with accompanying CD-ROM, which won a Firecracker Award in 1997. Both were finalists for a Lambda Book Award. Smukler has received fellowships in poetry from the New York Foundation for the Arts and the Astraea Foundation. Her work has appeared in numerous journals and anthologies including *Pucker Up, Gay and Lesbian Poetry in Our Time, The New Fuck You: Adventures in Lesbian Reading, Women On Women III,* and *The Zenith of Desire.*

tatiana de la tierra is a bi-lingual, bi-cultural writer and activista, born in Colombia, bred in Mayami, and currently in an MFA Creative Writing Program in El Paso, Tejas. Her writings have been published in journals and anthologies such as *The Second Coming, Queer View Mirror, Compañeras*, and *The Femme Mystique*. She is also a former editor of the Latina lesbian magazines *esto no tiene nombre* and *conmoción* and currently directs the Latina lesbian writers' web, la telaraña. Since writing and activism are intricately linked, she welcomes communication from all Latina lesbians via la telaraña, 2626 N. Mesa #273, El Paso, TX 79902.

Margaret Vandenburg, Ph.D., is the associate director of the writing program at Barnard College, and a lecturer in the English Department. Despite these academic proclivities, her real vocation is writing lesbian fiction, whatever that is.

Rachel Weaver has made a home for herself in Chicago, where she writes and performs her poetry.

Terry Wolverton is the author of the novel *Bailey's Beads*, which was a finalist in the American Library Association's Gay and Lesbian Book Awards for 1997, and *Black Slip*, a collection of poetry. She has also edited several anthologies including *Indivisible: Short Fiction by West Coast Gay and Lesbian Writers*, and both volumes one and two of *His: Brilliant New Fiction by Gay Men* and *Hers: Brilliant New Fiction by Lesbians*. Her fiction, poetry, essays and drama have been published in periodicals internationally.

Books from Cleis Press

LESBIAN AND GAY STUDIES

Chasing the American Dyke Dream: Homestretch
edited by Susan Fox Rogers.
ISBN: 1-57344-036-1 14.95 paper

The Case of the Good-For-Nothing Girlfriend
by Mabel Maney.
Lambda Literary Award Nominee.
ISBN: 0-939416-91-3 10.95 paper.

The Case of the Not-So-Nice Nurse by Mabel
Maney. Lambda Literary Award Nominee.
ISBN: 0-939416-76-X 9.95 paper.

Nancy Clue and the Hardly Boys in *A Ghost in
the Closet* by Mabel Maney.
Lambda Literary Award Nominee.
ISBN: 1-57344-012-4 10.95 paper.

Different Daughters: A Book by Mothers of Lesbians,
second edition, edited by Louise Rafkin.
ISBN: 1-57344-050-7 12.95 paper.

*Different Mothers: Sons & Daughters of Lesbians
Talk about Their Lives,* edited by Louise Rafkin.
Lambda Literary Award Winner.
ISBN: 0-939416-41-7 9.95 paper.

A Lesbian Love Advisor by Celeste West.
ISBN: 0-939416-26-3 9.95 paper.

On the Rails: A Memoir, second edition,
by Linda Niemann. Introduction by Leslie
Marmon Silko.
ISBN: 1-57344-064-7. 14.95 paper.

Queer Dog: Homo Pup Poetry, edited by Gerry
Gomez Pearlberg.
ISBN: 1-57344-071-X. 12.95. paper.

WRITER'S REFERENCE

*Putting Out: The Essential Publishing Resource
Guide For Gay and Lesbian Writers,*
fourth edition, by Edisol W. Dotson.
ISBN: 1-57344-033-7 14.95 paper.

DEBUT LITERATURE

Marianne Faithfull's Cigarette: Poems
by Gerry Gomez Pearlberg
ISBN: 1-57344-034-5 12.95 paper

Memory Mambo by Achy Obejas.
Lambda Literary Award Winner.
ISBN: 1-57344-017-5 12.95 paper.

*We Came All The Way from Cuba So You Could
Dress Like This? Stories* by Achy Obejas.
Lambda Literary Award Nominee.
ISBN: 0-939416-93-X 10.95 paper.

Seeing Dell by Carol Guess.
ISBN: 1-57344-023-X 12.95 paper.

WORLD LITERATURE

A Forbidden Passion by Cristina Peri Rossi.
ISBN: 0-939416-68-9 9.95 paper.

*Half a Revolution: Contemporary Fiction by Russian
Women,* edited by Masha Gessen.
ISBN 1-57344-006-X \$12.95 paper.

*The Little School: Tales of Disappearance and
Survival in Argentina* by Alicia Partnoy.
ISBN: 0-939416-07-7 9.95 paper.

Peggy Deery: An Irish Family at War
by Nell McCafferty.
ISBN: 0-939416-39-5 9.95 paper.

SEX GUIDES

Good Sex: Real Stories from Real People, second
edition, by Julia Hutton.
ISBN: 1-57344-000-0 14.95 paper.

*The New Good Vibrations Guide to Sex: Tips and
techniques from America's favorite sex-toy store*, second edition, by Cathy Winks and Anne Semans.
ISBN: 1-57344-069-8 21.95 paper.

The Ultimate Guide to Anal Sex for Women
by Tristan Taormino.
ISBN: 1-57344-028-0 14.95 paper.

SEXUAL POLITICS

Annie Sprinkle: Post Porn Modernist — My Twenty-Five Years as a Multimedia Whore by Annie Sprinkle.
ISBN: 1-57344-039-6 19.95 paper

Forbidden Passages: Writings Banned in Canada, introductions by Pat Califia and Janine Fuller. Lambda Literary Award Winner.
ISBN: 1-57344-019-1 14.95 paper.

Public Sex: The Culture of Radical Sex by Pat Califia.
ISBN: 0-939416-89-1 12.95 paper.

Real Live Nude Girl: Chronicles of Sex-Positive Culture by Carol Queen.
ISBN: 1-57344-073-6. 14.95 paper.

Sex Work: Writings by Women in the Sex Industry, edited by Frédérique Delacoste and Priscilla Alexander.
ISBN: 0-939416-11-5 16.95 paper.

Susie Bright's Sexual Reality: A Virtual Sex World Reader by Susie Bright.
ISBN: 0-939416-59-X 9.95 paper.

Susie Bright's Sexwise by Susie Bright.
ISBN: 1-57344-002-7 10.95 paper.

Susie Sexpert's Lesbian Sex World by Susie Bright.
ISBN: 0-939416-35-2 9.95 paper.

GENDER TRANSGRESSION

Body Alchemy: Transsexual Portraits by Loren Cameron. Lambda Literary Award Winner.
ISBN: 1-57344-062-0 24.95 paper.

Dagger: On Butch Women, edited by Roxxie, Lily Burana, Linnea Due.
ISBN: 0-939416-82-4 14.95 paper.

I Am My Own Woman: The Outlaw Life of Charlotte von Mahlsdorf, translated by Jean Hollander.
ISBN: 1-57344-010-8 12.95 paper.

PoMoSexuals: Challenging Assumptions about Gender and Sexuality edited by Carol Queen and Lawrence Schimel. Preface by Kate Bornstein.
ISBN: 1-57344-074-4 14.95 paper.

Sex Changes: The Politics of Transgenderism by Pat Califia.
ISBN: 1-57344-072-8 16.95 paper.

Switch Hitters: Lesbians Write Gay Male Erotica and Gay Men Write Lesbian Erotica, edited by Carol Queen and Lawrence Schimel.
ISBN: 1-57344-021-3 12.95 paper.

EROTIC LITERATURE

Best Gay Erotica 1998, selected by Christopher Bram, edited by Richard Labonté.
ISBN: 1-57344-031-0 14.95 paper.

Best Gay Erotica 1997, selected by Douglas Sadownick, edited by Richard Labonté.
ISBN: 1-57344-067-1 14.95 paper.

Best Gay Erotica 1996, selected by Scott Heim, edited by Michael Ford.
ISBN: 1-57344-052-3 12.95 paper.

Best Lesbian Erotica 1998, selected by Jenifer Levin, edited by Tristan Taormino.
ISBN: 1-57344-032-9 14.95 paper.

Best Lesbian Erotica 1997, selected by Jewelle Gomez, edited by Tristan Taormino.
ISBN: 1-57344-065-5 14.95 paper.

The Leather Daddy and the Femme: An Erotic Novel by Carol Queen.
ISBN: 1-57344-037-X 14.00 paper

Serious Pleasure: Lesbian Erotic Stories and Poetry, edited by the Sheba Collective.
ISBN: 0-939416-45-X 9.95 paper.

TRAVEL & COOKING

Betty and Pansy's Severe Queer Review of New York by Betty Pearl and Pansy.
ISBN: 1-57344-070-1 10.95 paper.

Betty and Pansy's Severe Queer Review of San Francisco by Betty Pearl and Pansy.
ISBN: 1-57344-056-6 10.95 paper.

Food for Life & Other Dish, edited by Lawrence Schimel.
ISBN: 1-57344-061-2 14.95 paper.

THRILLERS & DYSTOPIAS

Another Love by Erzsébet Galgóczi.
ISBN: 0-939416-51-4 8.95 paper.

Dirty Weekend: A Novel of Revenge by Helen
Zahavi.
ISBN: 0-939416-85-9 10.95 paper.

Only Lawyers Dancing by Jan McKemmish.
ISBN: 0-939416-69-7 9.95 paper.

The Wall by Marlen Haushofer.
ISBN: 0-939416-54-9 9.95 paper.

POLITICS OF HEALTH

The Absence of the Dead Is Their Way of Appearing
by Mary Winfrey Trautmann.
ISBN: 0-939416-04-2 8.95 paper.

Don't: A Woman's Word by Elly Danica.
ISBN: 0-939416-22-0 8.95 paper

Voices in the Night: Women Speaking About Incest,
edited by Toni A.H. McNaron and Yarrow
Morgan.
ISBN: 0-939416-02-6 9.95 paper.

*With the Power of Each Breath: A Disabled Women's
Anthology,* edited by Susan Browne, Debra
Connors and Nanci Stern.
ISBN: 0-939416-06-9 10.95 paper.

COMIX

Dyke Strippers: Lesbian Cartoonists A to Z, edited
by Roz Warren.
ISBN: 1-57344-008-6 16.95 paper.
*The Night Audrey's Vibrator Spoke: A Stonewall
Riots Collection* by Andrea Natalie.
Lambda Literary Award Nominee.
ISBN: 0-939416-64-6 8.95 paper.

*Revenge of Hothead Paisan: Homicidal Lesbian
Terrorist* by Diane DiMassa.
Lambda Literary Award Nominee.
ISBN: 1-57344-016-7 16.95 paper.

VAMPIRES & HORROR

Brothers of the Night: Gay Vampire Stories edited
by Michael Rowe and Thomas S. Roche.
ISBN: 1-57344-025-6 14.95 paper.

Dark Angels: Lesbian Vampire Stories, edited by
Pam Keesey. Lambda Literary Award Nominee.
ISBN 1-7344-014-0 10.95 paper.

Daughters of Darkness: Lesbian Vampire Stories,
edited by Pam Keesey.
ISBN: 0-939416-78-6 12.95 paper.

Vamps: An Illustrtated History of the Femme Fatale
by Pam Keesey.
ISBN: 1-57344-026-4 21.95.

*Sons of Darkness: Tales of Men, Blood and
Immortality,* edited by Michael Rowe and
Thomas S. Roche.
Lambda Literary Award Nominee.
ISBN: 1-57344-059-0 12.95 paper.

*Women Who Run with the Werewolves: Tales of
Blood, Lust and Metamorphosis,* edited by Pam
Keesey. Lambda Literary Award Nominee.
ISBN: 1-57344-057-4 12.95 paper.

 Since 1980, Cleis Press has
published provocative, smart
books—for girlfriends of all
genders. Cleis Press books are
easy to find at your favorite
bookstore—or direct from us! We welcome
your order and will ship your books as
quickly as possible. Individual orders must
be prepaid (U.S. dollars only). Please add
15% shipping. CA residents add 8.5% sales
tax. MasterCard and Visa orders: include
account number, exp. date, and signature.

How to Order
- **Phone:** 1-800-780-2279 or (415) 575-4700
  Monday–Friday, 9 am–5 pm PST
- **Fax:** (415) 575-4705
- **Mail: Cleis Press** P.O. Box 14684,
  San Francisco, California 94114
- **E-mail:** Cleis@aol.com